Books & Bindings

BOOKBINDING TERMS

Before we start with the different lessons, let's cover some basic terms you may come across in the instructions. Books are generally comprised of two covers and a spine.

Covers may be made of materials such as chipboard, book board, foam board, metal, wood, or clay to name just a few.

A Spine supports the book block and may or may not be made o ~~material as~~ the covers.

A Fore edge is the edge of the book opposite the spine. The top of the book is referred to as the head and the bottom as the tail.

A Gutter is the space between the cover and the spine that allows the book the flexibility to open and close.

End paper is the paper that connects the cover to the text block.

A Text Block is made up of signatures: ~~r~~oups of pages nested together for the pur~~p~~oses of sewing into a book.

GW00578087

Square Knot

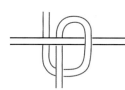

Handmade Books & Bindings presents updated tools and techniques that make this art form accessible to everyone!

Ancient History
Pages 15 - 17

Leather Journal
Pages 18 - 21

Poly Shrink Spirals
Pages 22 - 25

Pillow Books of Lady Otori
Pages 26 - 32

Travel Journal Trio
Pages 40 - 44

Nature Journal
Pages 45 - 46

Dream Journal
Pages 47 - 49

Rainbow Wish Book
Pages 50 - 51

Cutting Tools
Craft knives • X-Acto knife • Fiskars paper trimmers

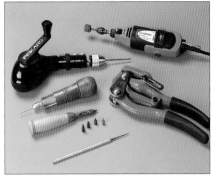

Hole Punching Tools
Dremel tool • Awls • Japanese screw punch • Hand drill

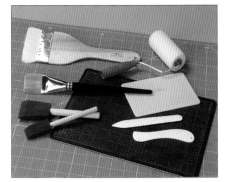

Applicators • Folders • Boards
Foam brushes • Brayer • Bristle brushes • Bone folders • Cutting boards

Rulers
Metal T-square • Quilter's ruler • Aluminum ruler with recessed foam backing

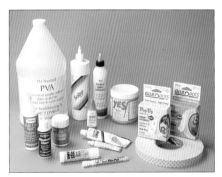

Adhesives
Glue sticks • PVA • Sobo • Yes! • E6000 • Gem-Tac • Quick Grab • Double-stick tape

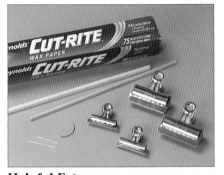

Helpful Extras
Waxed paper • Binder clips • Square dowels • Needles

BOOKBINDING TOOLS

While it isn't necessary to possess every tool known to the craft, it is helpful to have a few basics to make the art go smoothly. These can be broken down into a few categories: cutting and shaping tools, rulers, bone folders, and needles.

CUTTING AND SHAPING TOOLS

The most important of these is a good, sharp craft knife. These come in a variety of shapes and sizes. My favorite is the type with snap-off blades. I prefer this type because a fresh blade is always at hand and they are inexpensive to replace. A sharp blade is important for two reasons: to get a clean edge on the material you're cutting and to prevent injuries. When your blade is dull, you're much more likely to slip and cut yourself. Replace your blades often.

The question I get in class most often is, "How do you cut book board?" I prefer a Fiskars hand-held rotary cutter. It slices through even the thickest board with ease.

For cutting whole reams of paper, unless you want to invest in a guillotine paper cutter, which can run into the thousands of dollars, you can't beat a local print shop. They can usually do the job for just a few dollars while you wait. If you're cutting a few sheets at a time, I like the Fiskars desk rotary cutter. It comes in 12" and 24" models and is fairly precise, provided it's used properly. When cutting, it's important to put one hand on the paper you're cutting to prevent it from sliding away from the blade. I like this model because the blades and cutting surface are easily replaced when they wear out.

For miscellaneous cutting, drilling, sanding and finishing jobs, a Dremel tool is an excellent investment. This crafter's tool is found in hardware stores and comes with a myriad of attachments. The tools come in both cordless and corded models. If your budget only allows you one, I would choose a corded model since it affords more power, and nothing is more frustrating than waiting to finish a project while a battery recharges.

An awl is a sharp tool used for poking holes. They come in many sizes, so be sure to use a thin one so that your holes are the correct size. Also, be careful when using a graduated type that you don't make the hole too big by pushing too far. I prefer to use a jeweler's awl, because the needle is long and sharp. The handle and the needle are made of one piece of metal, so the needle won't come loose.

Many different types of hole-punching tools are available. I use a variety of them, but my favorite is the Japanese Screw Punch. This tool is basically a self-contained anywhere hole punch. It's lightweight and compact, and comes with bits ranging from 1 mm to 4 mm size holes. It can punch a hole in several sheets of paper at a time, and can punch through matboard, book board, craft metal and metal mesh. Its best feature is that it's not limited by the reach of traditional hole punches.

While we're talking about cutting tools, I should mention that a cutting board is an essential tool. They prevent damage to both your work surface and cutting blade. Choose the appropriate size for your needs and keep it on your work surface at all times. Most models have a 1" grid that can also be helpful in measuring and cutting on a 90-degree angle.

Covering Book Board

MATERIALS:
Book board, any dimension
2 pieces cover paper:
  1 piece 2" longer and wider than book board
  1 piece 1/2" shorter and narrower than book board

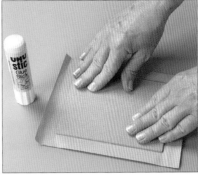

1. Apply adhesive to one side of board. Place face down, centered on larger piece of cover paper.

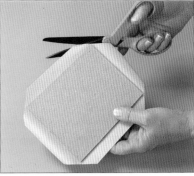

2. Miter all four corners, leaving a piece equal to the height of the board in each corner.

3. Put adhesive on one flap. Fold over, press into place, burnish with waxed paper. Press corner down using bone folder. Repeat for remaining three flaps.

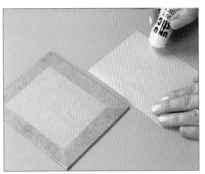

4. Apply adhesive to smaller piece of cover paper.

5. Center and adhere cover paper to the book board. Let dry completely.

RULERS

There are quite a few rulers that can do simple jobs well. I have a favorite that one of my students introduced me to a couple of years ago: a quilter's ruler. Olfa and Fiskars make two of the more common models. If I had a preference, it would be the Olfa brand because the yellow markings are easy on the eyes. This ruler comes in a variety of lengths and widths and it's the width that makes it so helpful. It enables you to measure and cut at the same time. If you don't have one, find one in a sewing notions department and ask a knowledgeable clerk to show you how it works. You'll be sold.

The only thing that is not ideal about a quilter's ruler is that since it's transparent by design, it can slip while you're cutting if you're not careful. If this is a problem for you, choose any of a variety of metal-edged rulers with a cork or foam backing. The drafting department of a craft store usually has an assortment. That's where I found my favorite: an aluminum ruler with recessed foam backing that allows the ruler to lie completely flush with the work surface. This feature prevents your knife from slipping under the edge of the ruler.

For heavy jobs such as cutting large pieces of book board, a long metal T square is necessary. The advantage of this type of ruler over a standard straightedge is that the T helps you attain a 90-degree angle more easily when you match it to the markings on a cutting mat.

BONE FOLDERS

A bone folder is a polymer-plastic tool made for scoring paper to make clean folds. It comes in a variety of lengths, sizes and shapes. I prefer a curved type with a thin flat tip that ends in a sharp point. It fits nicely in the hand and its thinly honed edge makes crisp folds in papers.

NEEDLES

Needles used in bookbinding are somewhat different than sewing needles. Ideally, they should have a slightly larger eye to accommodate heavy waxed linen threads but not so large as to widen the holes of the signature, thereby compromising the integrity of the structure. Rather than using large-eyed needles, flatten the end of the thread. Binder's needles tend to be slightly longer than sewing needles. This helps to get into tight spaces. I prefer round-tipped needles to sharps because I'm accident-prone. If your bookbinding needles are sharps, you can easily sand the tip off with sand paper or a Dremel tool. Some binders prefer curved needles, but I haven't found a stitch yet that requires one.

Other items I find useful that don't really fall into a particular category are waxed paper and blank newsprint. A wad of waxed paper acts as a great burnishing tool for covering book board and other glue tasks. It moves smoothly over the surface, removing wrinkles and flattening the paper without leaving marks. I work on a newsprint pad. It protects my work surface from inks, stains and glues. When one page is used, just tear it off and you have a fresh surface.

"The art of book binding, known as bibliopegy can be a great escape for any artist".

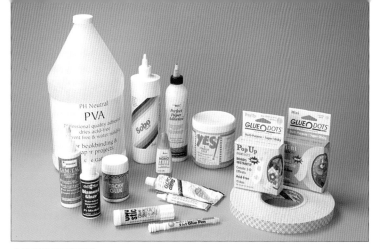

ADHESIVES

Another common question I hear in class is, "How do you know what type of glue to use for a particular job?" The short answer to that question is, "The least type of glue needed for the job." What does that mean? Glues can be classified in a number of ways, but I prefer to classify them in terms of stickiness. In other words, use only the level of stickiness necessary for the job. For the purposes of this book, I will only cover adhesives I use on a regular basis. However, there are many more on the market that will do different jobs well.

Level 1:

Glue stick - paper to cardstock, assuming it doesn't have to bear weight. Examples: Gluing two pages together or covering book board with thin paper. The advantage of a glue stick is that it's a fairly easy and dry application. This means less wrinkling or distortion of the paper. The disadvantage is that this type of glue is not as strong as others. So if you ask it to adhere a heavy paper or stand up to repeated openings and closings, it may fail. Keep the cap on when not in use or it may become too sticky to glide smoothly. I prefer the purple Uhu glue stick for its smoothness and the Purple color which dries clear and helps you see where you've applied it.

Level 2:

PVA - Polyvinyl acetate is a smooth white adhesive that dries clear. It's useful for binding heavy papers, boards or fabrics together. It will bear some weight but not heavy objects. I like to tell students that the biggest advantage is that it dries much faster than other white glues, and its biggest disadvantage is that it dries much faster than other white glues. In other words, if you know what you're doing and are focused, deliberate and steady, you'll love the speed with which this glue allows you to work. If you tend to make placement errors, it can be unforgiving. In the latter case, Sobo glue might be a better choice for you as it dries somewhat slower, allowing you the opportunity to rearrange at times. In either case, I suggest applying this type of glue with a soft bristle brush or sponge brush. It can be helpful to dip your brush in water before the glue to thin it a bit and allow your brush to flow more smoothly. For large areas, a sponge brayer can be a great tool since it puts on a thin, even layer very quickly. For small areas, I've been known to apply it with my finger because I'm too impatient to search for a brush.

Level 3:

Dimensional Adhesive - This type of adhesive is useful for adhering dimensional objects of varying sizes. It typically takes much longer to dry depending on the amount used and the size of the object to be adhered. A few examples are Gem-Tac, E6000 and Quick Grab. My favorite in this group is Gem-Tac for its inoffensive odor. Another recent addition to this list is a product called Glue Dots. These are small dabs of a very sticky adhesive that come on a paper roll. They come in several sizes. Surprisingly strong considering their size, they can hold small objects such as coins or charms with ease. Keep your fingers away from them, as they can be hard to remove.

Keep in mind that there are other methods for adhering heavy objects such as wiring or tying objects in place. If glue isn't doing the trick, consider another angle.

PREPARING SIGNATURES

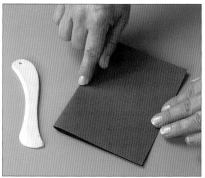

1. Fold text sheets in half one at a time. Press the sheets flat with a bone folder.

2. Nest in groups (signatures) per project instructions. Mark a T in pencil in the top right corner of each to signify the tops.

3. Prepare a punching pattern (jig) per project instructions.

4. Nest the jig inside the signature and punch holes with an awl according to pattern. Use a Davey board cradle if you have one or punch by hand.

Lost and Found

With every loss, there is a lesson to be found.

This little pamphlet book celebrates the process of learning how to be one's own self.

SIZE: 3⅜" x 3⅝"

MATERIALS:
1 piece 90 lb. watercolor paper 3⅝" x 13½"
1 piece map paper 2⅛" square
1 scrap map paper
1 piece map vellum 3⅝" x 6½"
5 pieces lost and found pages 3⅝" x 6½"
1 piece ⅛" ivory ribbon 18"

15" *Royalwood Ltd.* green waxed linen thread
1 compass
1 copper mesh heart
2 copper eyelets
1 copper jump ring
Various small beads

SUPPLIES: *Tsukineko* ink (Jet Black StazOn; Timber StazOn refill; Walnut ink: Java, Eucalyptus; Onyx Black Versafine; Versacolor cubes: Bark, Pinecone) • Sponge brush • Rubber stamps: *All Night Media* Jive alphabet; *Limited Edition* number; map) • ⅛" hole punch • Eyelet setter • Awl • Bookbinding needle • Alligator clip • Stiff Black sponge brush • Bone folder • Craft iron and Teflon craft sheet • Small butane torch • Glue stick • *Crafter's Pick* The Ultimate! craft glue

continued on pages 8-9

1. Flatten and press inked paper.

2. Punch hole in covers and signatures.

3. Thread ribbon through the hole in the cover.

Lost and Found

continued from page 7

INSTRUCTIONS:

Cover:

Take ½ teaspoon of Java walnut ink and dilute it with ¼ cup of water. Crumple the watercolor paper and flatten it out again. Lay it on a craft sheet and dab with the walnut ink. Iron the paper flat with a craft iron until it dries. Fold it in half and then again in quarters. Hint: When folding the second and third folds, don't fold quite to the center fold but leave a slight ¹⁄₁₆" gap. This will help the book to fold flat. With the two quarter folds on the inside, punch three ⅛" holes as follows: ⅛" from the spine edge while the book is closed and ⅛" from each fore edge. All three holes should be centered with the height of the book; they will accommodate the ribbon closure. Edge the 2⅛" map square with Bark and Pinecone inks. Adhere the square centered on the front cover. Tear a couple of small pieces from the map scrap. Edge and adhere to the front cover, wrapping around the top part of the spine and the bottom fore edge. Stamp "Lost and Found". Stamp a map stamp on the two inside flaps. Punch a ⅛" hole just above the top edge of the map, about ¾" from the left side of the map. Set a copper eyelet in the hole. Holding onto the copper mesh heart with an alligator clip, heat it with a butane torch to age it. Be careful not to overdo the heat or the copper will burn off. Punch a ⅛" hole in the top left side of the heart and set an eyelet in it. To age the compass, put a bit of Timber refill ink on a paper towel. Dab the ink onto the clear part of the compass gently to create an antique haze. Set aside to dry.

Sponge some Java walnut ink onto the ribbon. Iron dry. I also stamped the ribbon with a map stamp using Jet Black StazOn ink. Thread the ribbon as follows: from the outside of the front cover through the fore edge hole, out the first spine hole, back in the second spine hole and out the back fore edge hole.

With an awl, punch a small hole through the map on the front cover, just below the spot where the eyelet is set. Attach the copper heart with the jump ring. Adhere the compass with The Ultimate craft glue.

4. Dab with Eucalyptus Walnut ink and press signature papers.

Book Block:

First, you may want to age the papers with Eucalyptus walnut ink. Mix 1 teaspoon of ink to ¼ cup of water. Dab the ink on in spatters with a stiff sponge brush. You can just let it dry or iron the spatters using a craft iron and craft sheet. Edge the pages with Bark and Pinecone inks. After you bring the color to the desired shade, decorate the pages with rubber stamps.

Nest the blank pages and stamp each line on a single page (beginning with the front page) as follows:

I lost my youth
And found wisdom
I lost my way
And found a new path
I lost my energy
And found my strength
I lost my heart
And found my true love
I lost my nerve
And found my courage
I lost my patience
And found understanding
I lost my mind
And found my sense of humor
I lost my temper
And found serenity
I lost my innocence
And found my lust for life
With every loss, time has taught me there is a lesson
    to be found.

Fold the vellum map page in half and nest the book block inside it. It will be your signature wrap. Nest the book block inside the cover and punch 3 holes using an awl through all the layers. One should be in the center and will go right through the ribbon on the cover, one about ⅜" from the head of the book and the last ⅜" from the tail.

Sewing the book:

Thread your needle with the waxed linen thread. Begin on the outside at the head of the book. Insert your needle and pull the thread through, leaving a 4" tail. Exit the book at the middle hole. Your needle will go through the ribbon. Go back into the book at the bottom hole and come out through the middle hole. Tie off with a square knot at the head of the book. Thread the beads on the ends of each thread and knot to secure. Tie the ribbon closed at the fore edge of the book.

Thanks to my friend Leslie McFarlane for her inspiration on this project.

Gray dots (1/16" from edges and folds) indicate ribbon holes. Black dots (at center back) indicate where cover and signatures are bound together.

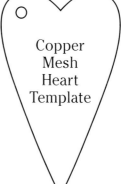

Copper Mesh Heart Template

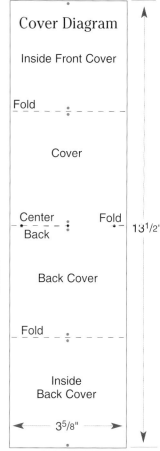

Cover Diagram

Inside Front Cover

Fold

Cover

Center Back   Fold

Back Cover

Fold

Inside Back Cover

13½"

3⅝"

5. Decorate and ink edges.

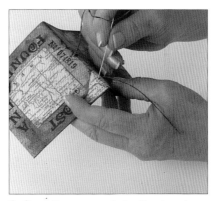

6. Sew the pages into the book.

7. Age copper with a heat gun.

1. Twist wire around a toothpick to form a loop.

2. Glue ribbon to back cover. Glue closure over the ribbon.

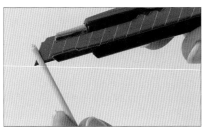

3. Cut a slit in the toothpick with a craft knife.

4. Feed the ribbon through the slit and glue a bead in place.

5. Stamp and decorate accordion panel.

6. Fold accordion panel.

French Accordion Book Pin

Have you ever thought of turning a book into wearable art? Attach a pin back and presto, your book becomes an artsy accessory. Thanks to my friend Terry Whinery for her inspiration for this project.

SIZE:
Antique Justice: 1¼" x 2½"
Postage Stamp: 1¼" x 1½"

MATERIALS:
2 pieces matboard 1¼" x 2½"	1 piece wire 3"
2 pieces cover paper 3" x 4"	1 toothpick
1 piece text paper 2½" x 11"	1 closure bead
1 pin back	3 ribbon beads

SUPPLIES:
Dye-based stamp pads • Stipple brush • French or travel theme stamps and postage stamps • Bone Folder • Sharp craft knife • Small art piece for the cover • Dimensional glue such as Gem-Tac • Glue stick • Optional: Metallic rub-ons • Nylon bead threader • *Gildenglitz* leafing adhesive • Bark ink cube

INSTRUCTIONS:

Begin by covering the matboards with cover paper. (Instructions on page 5.)

To prepare the closure wire, wrap the center of the wire around the toothpick and twist to form a loop. Using a dimensional glue, adhere the ribbon closure so that the full length of ribbon falls to the right side of the inside of the back cover. Glue the wire on top of the ribbon so that the loop protrudes from the right side of the board. Allow to dry.

Meanwhile, cut a ¼" vertical slit in the toothpick about 1" from the pointed tip. This is tricky so take your time. You may have to make a few cuts to get all the way through. Afterward, use a dark bronze metallic rub-on to color the wood. Set it aside to dry.

Stamp the paper strip in French or travel theme stamps. Add Gildenglitz and edge the sides with a Bark ink pad. Stipple if desired. Take your paper and fold in half, quarters and eighths to get an 8-panel accordion piece.

Adhere the front flap of the accordion panel to the front cover and the back flap to the back cover. (Be sure the glue is dry on the wire/ribbon closure.)

Using a bead threader, thread the ribbon through the slit in the toothpick. The ribbon should be straight with no twists and the tip of the toothpick should be facing the bottom of the book. Slide the toothpick up to the book and make a knot in the ribbon at 3¼" from the book to keep the closure in place. Glue a large-hole bead to the top of the toothpick. Slide the toothpick down to the knot. Thread the 3 other beads onto the end of the ribbon and knot to secure.

The ribbon wraps around the back of the book and then across the front. Slip the toothpick through the wire loop to secure. Glue the pin back to the back of the book if you want to wear it as a pin.

He Said, She Said:
A Couple's Travel Journal

Have you been searching for a unique gift for a newly wed couple? He said, She said: A Couple's Travel Journal provides a wonderful place to record all those precious "firsts we shared on the honeymoon". The envelopes inside will keep those ticket stubs and little trinkets safe.

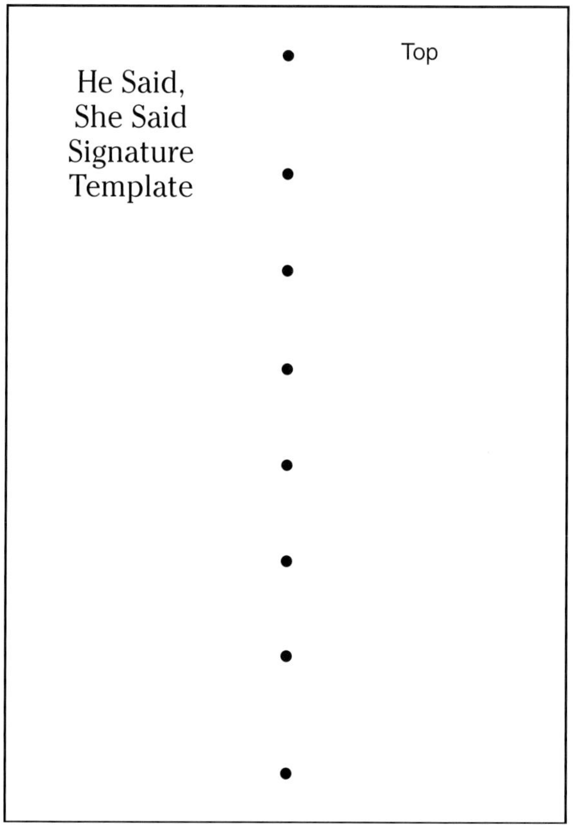

SIZE: 4½" x 5¾" x 1½"

MATERIALS:

2 pieces book board 4½" x 5⅝"
1 piece book board 4½" x 5½"
2 pieces book board ¾" x 4½"
1 piece leather 6" x 10½"
1 piece fabric 6" x 10½"
40 pieces mauve text paper 4¼" x 11"
32 pieces moss text paper 4¼" x 11"
4 pieces end paper 4¼" x 11"
2 Kraft envelope templates
2 cream envelope labels
1 piece moss ribbon 12"
1 piece burgundy ribbon 12"
Brass lock and key charms
1 piece 4 cord moss waxed linen thread 1½ yards

1 piece 4 cord antique rose waxed linen thread 1½ yards
2 pieces Buckram 3" x 4"
1 piece 2" ivory cotton headband
2 signature hole-punching templates
2 pieces Tyvek ¾" x ¾"
2 paper label holders
4 brass eyelets
1 piece burgundy cover label
1 piece Kraft cover label

He Said, She Said Signature Template

Top

SUPPLIES: Background writing stamp such as *Penny Black* Letter Background • Inkpads(*Marvy* #18 Brown # #13 Ochre; *Cat's Eye* Chestnut Roan; *Ranger* Adirondack Caramel) • Stipple brush • Gold leaf pen • Optional but helpful: 3/16" wooden spacers • Waxed paper for burnishing • Metal ruler • Craft knife • Bone folder • Pencil • Scissors • Cutting board • Eyelet setter • Hammer • Awl • PVA glue and glue brush

INSTRUCTIONS:

Preparing the text blocks:

Fold the mauve text papers in half and nest in groups of 5 sheets each to make 8 signatures. Use a bone folder to press a crisp fold in each sheet. Make a T in the top right-hand corner of each signature to signify the top. Cut out the hole-punching template and fold it down the center. Nest it inside the 1st signature with the Ts matching and punch the holes according to the pattern. Repeat for the other 7 signatures. Repeat this procedure for the moss text papers. Adjust the number of pages in each signature if necessary to make each text block the same thickness.

Sewing the text blocks:

This stitch is a classic codex stitch. Thread your needle with the antique rose waxed linen thread. For clarity of instructions, the holes will be numbered from head to tail with numbers 1-8 as shown in **Fig. 1**.

Begin on the outside of the spine in the 1st hole of the 1st mauve signature. Enter the 1st hole and pull the thread through, leaving a 6" tail. Sew to the tail of the book using a running stitch: come out at the 2nd hole, go back in at the 3rd, come out at the 4th, go back in at the 5th, come out at the 6th, in at the 7th and back out at the 8th, or last hole.

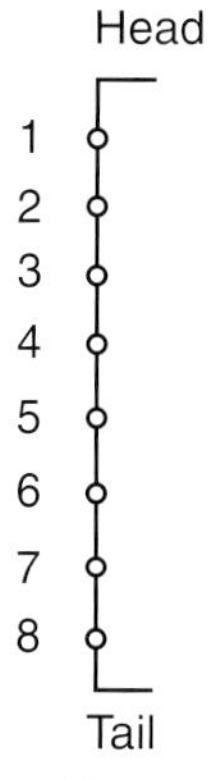

Add the 2nd signature next to the first, making sure the Ts match. You might find bulldog clips to be useful to hold the signatures together while you stitch. Enter the spine at the 8th hole of the 2nd signature and come back out at the 7th hole. Instead of doing a running stitch to the top of the 2nd signature, go back into the 1st signature at the 7th hole and exit the 1st signature at the 6th hole. Now enter the 2nd signature at the 6th hole and exit at the 5th hole. Re-enter the 1st signature at the 5th hole and exit at the 4th hole. Enter the 2nd signature at the 4th hole and exit at the 3rd hole. Re-enter the 1st signature at the 3rd hole and exit at the 2nd hole. Enter the 2nd signature at the 2nd hole and exit at the 1st hole. At this point connect the 1st and 2nd signatures with a square knot (right thread over left, then left over right). This modified running

Head

1
2
3
4
5
6
7
8

Tail

Fig. 1

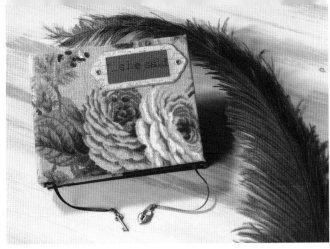

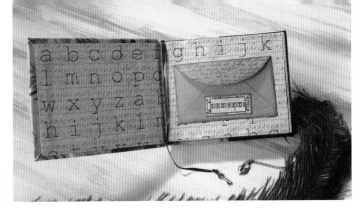

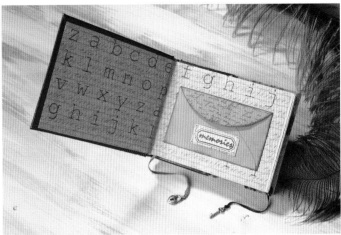

He Said, She Said - continued from page 12

stitch is the codex stitch. Add the 3rd signature next to the 2nd signature, making sure that the Ts match. Proceed to the tail of the book with the codex stitch. When you exit the tail of the book at the 8th hole, connect the 2nd and 3rd signatures with a kettle stitch. To do a kettle stitch, insert your needle into the thread that connects the 1st and 2nd signatures at the 8th hole. Pull the thread until a loop forms and insert your needle into that loop. Pull until snug.

Continue adding signatures, sewing with the codex stitch and connecting each signature to the previous one with a kettle stitch. End with a double kettle stitch.

For gluing the spine, it helps hold the book block upright if you attach 2 binder clips to the fore-edge at the head and tail – the book will balance on the wings of the clips. After the sewing is finished, apply PVA glue to the spine using a glue brush. Center the Buckram over the spine and press into place. The Buckram will be a little bit shorter than the spine. Do not fold the sides of the Buckram over, but leave them out like wings while the glue sets. Tap some more glue on top. Wrap one end of the burgundy ribbon around a piece of Tyvek. Apply glue to the Tyvek and place it about halfway down the spine. **See Fig 2**. Loop the long end of the ribbon over the head of the book. Cut the headband into four ½" pieces. Glue one piece on the spine at the head of the book so that the white ridge of the headband protrudes slightly over the edge and covers the folds of the signatures. Glue another piece on the spine at the tail in the same manner. Set the first book block aside to dry. Repeat this entire sewing and gluing procedure with the

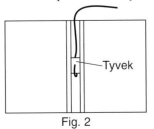

Fig. 2

moss signatures. Set that book block aside to dry also while you construct the cover assembly.

Constructing the covers:

The cover board measuring 5½" wide is the common cover shared by both books. Measure halfway across this board 2¾" and mark a line from head to tail on both sides of the board. Lay the fabric face down horizontally in front of you and draw a pencil line ¾" from the left edge and ¾" up from the bottom edge. Apply PVA glue to one of the cover boards measuring 5⅝" wide and lay this board horizontally in the corner where the two lines intersect. Burnish with a wad of waxed paper on the fabric side to insure a smooth application. If you have a ³⁄₁₆" spacer, lay it down to the right of the first board. If you don't have a spacer, measure ³⁄₁₆" to the right of the board and mark a line with a pencil. Apply PVA glue to the spine piece and lay it down on the fabric to the right of the spacer, or pencil mark. Burnish with waxed paper. Lay the spacer down to the right of the spine piece. Using the marked cover board, apply PVA glue to half of the board – to ¼" beyond the pencil mark. Lay this board down next to the spacer. Burnish well. Miter the corners, leaving an amount of fabric in each corner equal to the height of the book board. Apply PVA glue to the end flap and wrap around the book board. Since the fabric is so stiff, you will have to apply some pressure for as much as a minute or so to get the fabric to stick to the board. Apply PVA glue to the bottom flap and wrap it over the board. Repeat for the upper flap.

What you have now is the fabric front cover and spine and half of the shared cover. The next step is to add the leather front cover and spine and to finish the shared cover. Lay the leather in front of you wrong side up. Make a pencil line ¾" up from the bottom edge all the way across the leather. Turn the fabric-covered assembly that you've just finished to the wrong side. Apply PVA glue to half of the shared cover board from the pencil line to the unfinished end. Note that this is not the fabric-covered side, but the side with only the flaps showing and that you are applying glue away from the fabric covered part. Only two small parts of the fabric flaps will have glue on them. Lay this glued half of the shared cover on the right edge of the leather. The pencil line on the cover board will be even with the right edge of the leather and the bottom edge of the assembly will lay on the pencil line you've drawn on the leather.

instructions continued on page 14

Note that the fabric cover is face up for this step, and that the leather and fabric will be on opposite sides of the cover. The end papers will cover the remaining exposed sides of the book board at the end of the binding.

Refer to **Fig 3**. Continue laying out and gluing the cover as follows: lay a spacer to the left of the shared cover board. Apply PVA glue to the

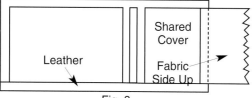

Fig. 3

remaining spine piece and place it next to the spacer. Burnish well. Move the spacer to the left of the spine piece. Apply PVA glue to the last cover board and lay it next to the spacer. Burnish well. Trim the remaining leather on the left edge to ¾". Miter the corners, apply glue to one flap at a time beginning with the end flap and wrap around the cover. The leather may be slippery and require that you hold it in place until the glue sets – as long as a minute or so. Now your cover assembly is complete.

Gluing the text blocks to the covers:

Beginning with the mauve book block, apply PVA glue to the outside of the entire piece of Buckram. Place the block centered inside the spine of the fabric cover. Note that the leather cover will be face up and to your right when you insert the first book block. Be sure the ribbon bookmark is at the head of the book before setting the block down. Press the Buckram into place. Use a bone folder to press both sides into the gutters. After a brief drying time of a few minutes, place a piece of waxed paper on each side of the book block and close the fabric book. Repeat this procedure, adding the moss book block to the leather side of the book. When both sides have had some time to dry, you will add the end papers.

Adding the end papers:

Apply glue to the first end paper and adhere it to the inside of one cover, beginning ⅛" in from the fore-edge of the cover, centered top to bottom. Smooth the paper as you go to eliminate any wrinkles or bubbles. Press it into the gutter before smoothing it onto the text block. Burnish with a wad of waxed paper. Trim the right edge if necessary. Repeat this procedure with the other three end papers.

Adding the embellishments:

Thread the key charm on the moss ribbon and knot in place. Thread the locket charm on the burgundy ribbon and knot in place. Trim the envelopes, score and glue the three lower flaps. Stamp a background writing stamp on the outside of each top flap in Brown ink. Edge the envelopes with a Chestnut Roan Cat's Eye. Trim the memories label, stipple with Adirondack Caramel ink, edge with a gold leaf pen and affix to the bottom of one of the envelopes with double-stick mounting tape. Attach the envelope to the inside cover of the leather book using a glue stick. Trim the secrets label, stipple, edge with a gold leaf pen and affix to the bottom of the other envelope. Attach to inside cover of the fabric book.

Stipple both label holders using Marvy #13

Ochre ink. Edge with a Chestnut Roan Cat's Eye. Stamp with a background writing stamp. Set eyelets in the holes. Trim 'he said' and 'she said' labels and glue to label holders, or prepare and insert your own labels if you prefer. Affix label holders to covers using glue dots.

BOOK BLOCK, BUCKRAM, LEATHER, FABRIC, PAPERS AND COVERS

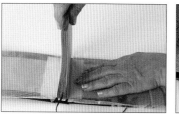

1. Sew book blocks.

2. Adhere buckram to book block to make a binding.

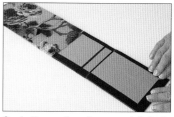

3. Adhere leather and fabric to book boards.

4. Adhere blocks to covers.

5. Glue end papers in place.

6. Glue labels to covers.

Top

Ancient
History
Journal
Spine
Template

· ·
· ·
· ·
· ·
· ·
· ·

Top

Ancient
History
Journal
Hole-Punching
Signature
Template

Fold

Ancient History Journal

Journal on pages 16-17

SIZE: 4½" x 7½" x 1"

MATERIALS:
2 pieces book board 4¼" x 7½"
2 pieces cover paper 6¼" x 9½"
2 pieces end paper 4" x 7¼"
3 spine tapes 1½" x 7"
32 pieces text paper 7¼" x 8¼"
3 yards *Royalwood Ltd.* black
    waxed linen thread

3 antique Mah Jong tiles
Spine hole-punching template
Signature hole-punching template
Copper Metallic Rub-Ons
ColorBox Cat's Eye Burnt Copper

SUPPLIES: 1 piece foam core board • Binding
needle • Bone folder • Awl • Scissors • Sponge
brush • *Hermafix* temporary bond • PVA glue

1. Smudge the cover with Copper Metallic RubOns.

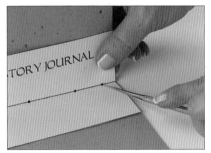

2. Punch holes in the signatures using a template.

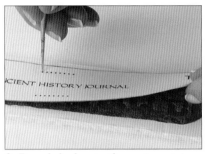

3. Punch holes in the spine strips.

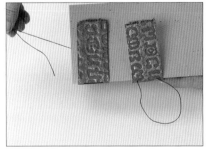

4. Sew spine strips to the signatures.

5. Glue cover strips to cover and embellish.

Ancient History Journal

continued from page 15

This textured journal features a simple to sew binding that allows the book to lie flat on the table. Eight signatures give you plenty of practice sewing the binding, and your book will have plenty of pages for you to fill.

INSTRUCTIONS:

Covering the book boards:

Cover the book boards with the cover papers, using PVA glue and a sponge brush. Gently smudge the bubble texture of the paper with Copper Metallic Rub-Ons to bring out the detail of the paper. Apply glue to the end papers and adhere to the inside covers.

Signatures:

Fold the text papers in half to form sheets $4\frac{1}{8}$" x $7\frac{1}{4}$". Nest in 8 signatures of 4 sheets each. Mark each signature with a T in the top right hand corner to signify the top. Trim the signature hole-punching template and score down the middle. Fold it in half and nest it inside the first signature, making sure to match up the Ts. Punch 6 holes in the signature according to the template using an awl. Repeat for the other 7 signatures.

Spine:

Trim the spine hole-punching template. Put a strip of Hermafix down the back of the template. Attach the template to 1of the spine strips. Punch 2 rows of 8 holes in the strip, using a piece of foam core board to aid in punching. Repeat for the other 2 strips. If you would like a rough edge on the spine strips, tear them and edge with Burnt Copper ink. Note: The spine strips need to be made of a very strong and durable material since they are the only parts of the book that connect the covers to the book block. If the material you want to use does not meet this criteria, you may want to sandwich a piece of Tyvek between 2 sheets of the material you're using to assure a solid structure.

Sewing is easy. Each signature attaches to 3 strips by a simple stitch. Lay the firstst strip along the spine at the top so that the first holes in the strip line up with the first 2 holes in the spine. Start on the inside of the signature at the top hole. Insert your needle

through the 1st hole of the signature and pull the thread through, leaving a 3" tail. Re-enter the 2nd hole and tie off inside with a square knot. Repeat 3 times per signature for all 8 signatures, taking care to match the Ts of all the signatures.

Insert the front cover between strips and the text block. Apply PVA glue to the first strip and adhere it to the cover. Repeat for the other 2 strips and then for strips on the back cover.

templates on page 15

Leather Journal

Create your own book of blank pages or print something special on decorative papers. Then tear the edges and bind the pages into a leather book of your very own making. A hole-punch pattern for the front cover is given, but you can personalize this book by creating your own design.

This binding is made with a simple running stitch, making this a good project for the novice bookbinder.

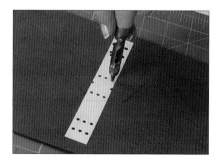

1. Punch holes in the spine.

SIZE: 4½" x 7" x 1"

MATERIALS:
7" x 10" leather
6½" x 9½" decorative paper
30 sheets text paper 8½" x 11"
1 spine hole-punching template
1 cover hole-punching template
3" x 6" cardstock for signature hole-punching template
24" suede strip
48" hemp thread
6 small wooden beads
2 large wooden beads

SUPPLIES: Binder's needle • Japanese screw punch • Cutting mat • Metal ruler • Bone folder • Scissors awl • PVA glue

INSTRUCTIONS:

Preparing the cover:

Trim the spine hole punching template. Lay the leather face down in front of you with the 10" measurement laying horizontally. Using PVA glue, adhere the template in the center of the leather with holes facing toward you. You'll have ¼" of leather showing above and below the guide. The center of the guide should be 5" from either edge. Punch all 20 holes with a screw punch. Clamp the cover template onto the front of the leather on the right side and punch the cover holes.

Spread a thin layer of PVA glue on top of the spine guide and glue the decorative paper face up centered over the template. Let it dry for a few minutes and then punch holes in the liner to match the holes in the cover and spine using an awl.

instructions continued on page 20
templates on page 21

Leather Journal

continued from page 18-19

Preparing the text papers:

The style of this journal is meant to be rustic, so rather than cutting the text papers to size, I suggest tearing them using a straight edge such as a metal-edged ruler and a cutting mat with 1" markings. Tear them on all 4 sides to make a final size of 6" x 8". I tore them in groups of 3 sheets at a time. This is a time-consuming step but worth the trouble.

After tearing the pages to size, fold them in half and nest them in 6 signatures of 5 sheets each. Label each signature with a T in the top right corner to signify the top.

Fold the cardstock in half lengthwise to make a spine hole-punching template. Lay the fold centered vertically along a row of holes punched in the spine and make 6 marks along the fold to match the sewing holes. Mark a T in the top right corner of the template you've made. Taking care to match the T of the template with the Ts of the signatures, nest the template inside the signatures one at a time and punch the holes according to the template.

Before beginning the sewing, thread the suede cord through the 2 holes at the edge of the 18 sewing holes. Go from the outside of the cover to the inside and back out the other hole. The cord should extend about 10" from the front hole and 13" from the back hole. This will allow the closure to knot at the front of the cover evenly.

Sewing the Signatures:

The closed cover will be placed on the table with the spine facing you, the head of the book to your left and the tail to your right. There are 3 horizontal sets of holes in the spine and 6 signatures. This means that 2 signatures will be attached to each row of holes. Holes will be numbered from 1-6 going from head to tail. You will be sewing the book from back to front: from the 6th to the 1st signature instead of the reverse.

Begin by threading your needle with the hemp cord. Insert the 6th signature, keeping the Ts at the top of the book, into the cover aligned with the last row of holes: the holes nearest the table. From the outside of the spine, insert the needle into the 6th (bottom) hole of the cover and 6th signature, pulling the thread through and leaving a 6" tail. This is a simple Running stitch so the needle will go into the spine and signature at the 6th hole, come out at the 5th hole, go back in at the 4th hole and so on until you exit the top (1st) hole. At this point, thread 1 of the small wooden beads onto the hemp and go back into the same hole of the spine. Do not go into the same signature but instead, add the 5th signature next to the 6th signature and insert the needle into the 1st hole of that signature. Using a running stitch, sew the 5th signature into the same row of holes in which you sewed the 6th signature. Exit the spine at the 6th hole and pull the thread snugly. Thread a bead on and go back through the spine. Add the 4th signature next to the 5th signature. Insert the needle from the outside of the 6th hole of this signature, exit the signature at the 5th hole and go through the spine at the 5th hole of the middle set of holes in the spine. Continue sewing with a running stitch until you exit the top hole. Thread a bead and re-enter the spine through the same hole. Add the 3rd signature next to the 4th signature and insert the needle into the 1st hole of that signature.

Continue in this manner, using the running stitch, adding beads at the top and bottom of each row of holes until you reach the 6th hole of the 1st signature. Thread a bead and insert the needle through the same hole of the cover. Tie a knot, pulling the thread snugly to tighten. Put a drop of PVA glue on the knot and trim the hemp to ½". Tie and glue a knot in the tail from the beginning.

Thread the large wooden beads onto the ends of the closure suede and knot. Tie the suede closed on the front cover. If you want to age your leather a bit, try using a piece of fine sandpaper on the edges. This will give your journal a weathered appearance.

templates on page 21

Step 1 on page 18

2. Clamp outer template to the front of book and punch holes.

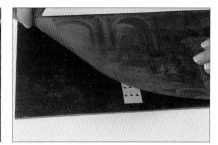

3. Adhere end papers inside the leather.

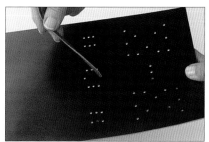

4. Thread suede cord through spine holes.

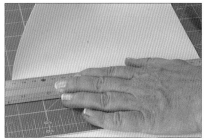

5. Tear text papers to size.

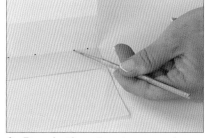

6. Punch the signatures using a template.

7. Sew the book using a Running Stitch.

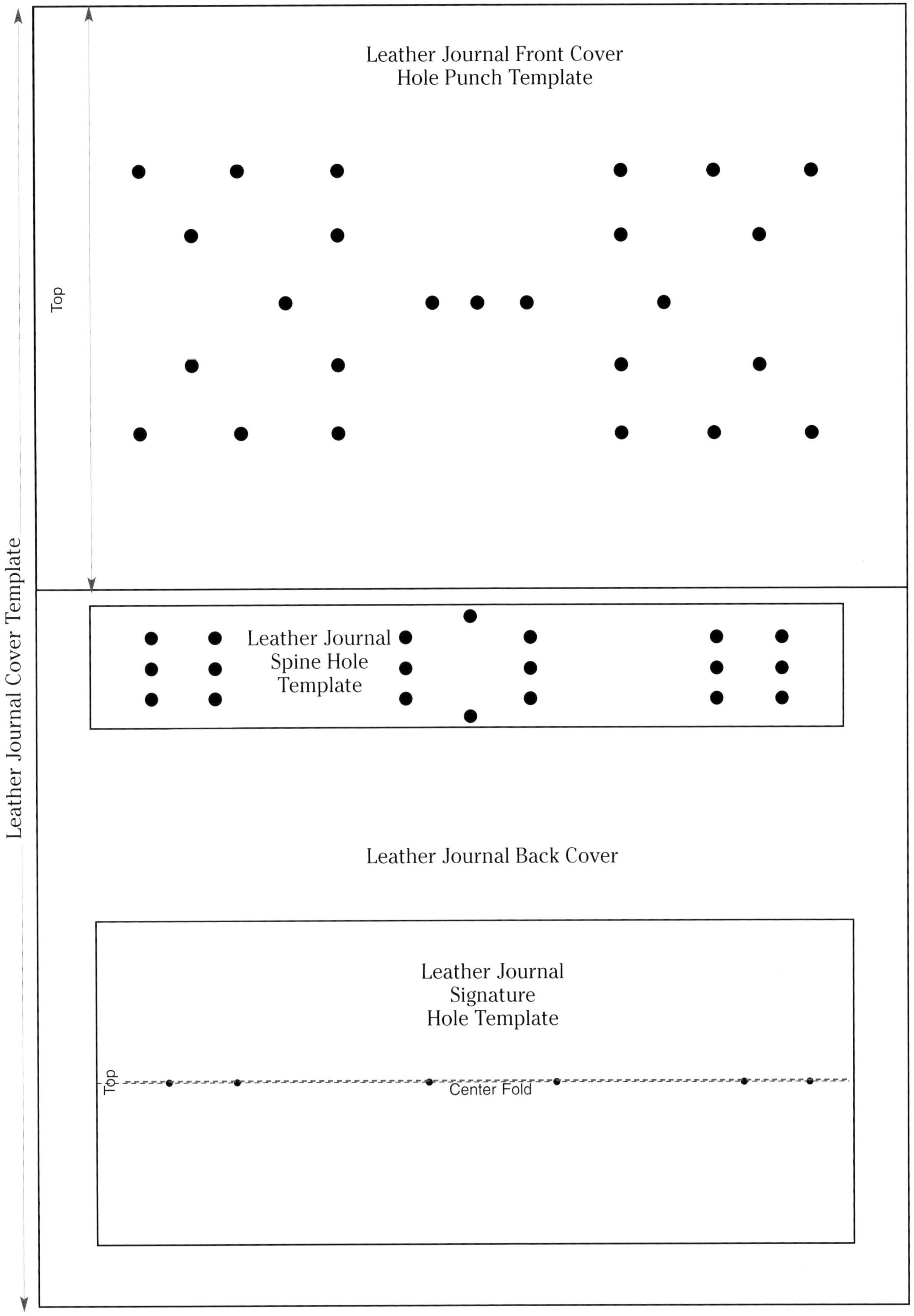

Leather Journal Front Cover
Hole Punch Template

Leather Journal Cover Template

Top

Leather Journal
Spine Hole
Template

Leather Journal Back Cover

Leather Journal
Signature
Hole Template

Top

Center Fold

Poly Shrink Spirals

"Art enables us to find ourselves and lose ourselves at the same time." This quote by Thomas Merton is just one of the reminders inside the Dream-Discover-Destiny pendant book.

These little books also allow you to keep a collection of photos close to your heart. Thanks to my friend Pam Sparks for her inspiration for this project.

SIZE: 1" x 1¼"

MATERIALS:

Text weight paper for pages
1 piece black shrink plastic
1 yard leather cord
8" of 26 gauge wire
Seed beads for spiral embellishment
1 charm
2 jump rings

1 glass bead
2 metal beads
1 piece 320 grit sandpaper or poly shrink sanding block
1 piece chipboard
1 skewer

SUPPLIES: *ColorBox* Crafter's Ink, *Tsukineko* Fabrico Ink, or Versacolor ink (Black or deep colors) • Mechanical pencil • Various colors metallic acrylic paint (not Lumiere) • Several cosmetic sponges • Scissors • Craft knife • Cutting mat • Hole punches (⅛", 1⁄16") • Jeweler's tools (Pliers, wire cutters) • Optional corner rounder

instructions continue on pages 24 - 25

Imagination is more important than knowledge.

-Albert Einstein

Poly Shrink
Cover
Template

Poly Shrink Spirals

continued from pages 20-21

INSTRUCTIONS:

Making the Covers:

Begin by sanding the entire piece of black shrink plastic on one side in a crosshatch pattern. Make a cover template by cutting a piece of chipboard to size: in this case 2¼" x 3". Draw a line ⅛" in from one of the 3" sides. Make marks along the line at the following points: ½", 1", 1½", 2", 2½". Using a ⅛" hole punch, punch a hole at each of those marks.

Use template to trace the outside edge onto the sanded shrink plastic. It is only necessary to mark the holes in half of the covers, since both covers in a set will be punched at the same time to insure accuracy. Keep in mind that shrink plastic does not shrink equally in both directions. This means that covers oriented vertically on the shrink plastic must be paired together and covers oriented horizontally must be paired together. If you do not remember to do this, your covers that are decorated as a pair will go into the oven matching but will not come out of the oven matching in size and shape. This is important!

After you cut out your covers and have them matched into pairs with shiny sides together, punch ⅛" holes in each pair of covers according to the pattern.

1. Sand shrink plastic in a crisscross pattern.

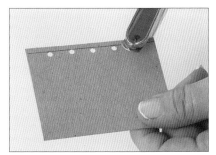

2. Punch holes in cover template.

3. Trace the template onto the sanded plastic.

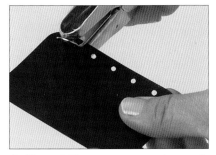

4. Round the corners and punch the holes.

Round the corners if desired, punching both covers at the same time to insure a perfect match. It can be tricky to line up such small pieces, so be sure you take your time on this step.

Decorate Covers:

Metallic acrylic paint makes an excellent base for shrink plastic art. When the plastic shrinks, it results in an almost suede-like quality. For some reason, Lumiere paint does not work as well as inexpensive paints such as Folk Art or Accent, perhaps because it is so much thicker than the less expensive brands. The colors will intensify and deepen when the plastic shrinks, so choose lighter shades of acrylic paint so that your stamping will show up well.

Pour a little paint into a shallow dish or plate. Using a cosmetic sponge, dab a thin layer onto the sanded sides of each pair. You may use more than one color on each cover if desired but thin layers are critical to a smooth result. After the first coat is dry, you may add another thin coat. When that layer dries, stamp images desired using any of the inks listed in the materials list. Be sure to use high contrast colors so the images will show up well after shrinking.

Handling the plastic by the edges to avoid smudging, place the covers on a piece of chipboard with each cover facing the same direction. Place the chipboard in a preheated 325-degree oven. The shrink plastic will curl and contort as it shrinks, but will flatten out when finished. Remove the chipboard from the oven and flatten the pieces completely using a piece of wood such as a rubber stamp mount. Let the covers cool completely. If you have paint on the reverse side of the covers, a little nail polish remover will get it off after it's baked. Trying to remove it prior to baking is easier but often results in damage to the opposite side as well, so I usually wait until it's baked to clean up smudges.

Preparing the Text:

Cut 12 text pages using the cover as a template. It is necessary to trace each cover individually because each cover will shrink a little differently and you want the pages to be the correct size and shape to fit the book.

Align1 of the pages with the front cover, both facing the same direction. With a mechanical pencil, mark the holes on the first page. Punch five $1/16"$ holes, 4 pages at a time using the pencil marks as a guide. Repeat for the other 8 pages, using a punched page as a guide. Round the corners 4 pages at a time also. If you want to add any embellishment to the pages, the time to do it is now, before assembly. Stack the pages in desired order and sandwich them between front and back covers.

Assembling the Book:

With all of the holes aligned, insert the wire from front to back at the bottom hole, leaving a tail in the back of about 1". Lay the skewer along the spine. Wrap the wire over the skewer and thread back through the same hole. This may take a little wiggling but it will go through. Pull the wire snugly. Thread 5 seed beads onto the wire and thread the wire through the next hole. Repeat this until the first 4 holes are threaded. On the last hole, wrap the wire and slip a jump ring on without adding beads before threading through the hole. Cut the wire off, leaving about 1". Pull the skewer out and wrap the beginning and ending wires a couple of times around the nearest loop before cutting off the remainder. Add a jump ring and charm to the bottom loop. Thread about 1 yard of cord through the top jump ring and center the book on it. Thread a metal bead, a glass bead and another metal bead over both ends of the cord and pull down to the jump ring to secure the book in the center of the cord. Tie the ends of the cord in an overhand knot or tie 2 slip knots to form an adjustable cord.

Of course, any size book can be made this way. Poly shrink shrinks about 55% of the original size so make sure you measure accordingly.

5. Stamp plastic.

6. Bake to shrink plastic.

7. Assemble the book.

```
┌─────────────────────────┐
│           Top           │
│                         │
│            ●            │
│                         │
│                         │
│      ● Pillow Book      │
│       Inner Binding     │
│         Template        │
│                         │
│            ●            │
│                         │
│                         │
│            ●            │
│                         │
│                         │
└─────────────────────────┘
```

The Pillow Books of Lady Otori

These traditional Japanese stab-bound books are known as 'makurabon' or pillow books due to their size and shape. They are made from half size oblong sheets of text paper. Traditional Japanese books were either written with a calligraphy brush or printed with a wood block, requiring soft, absorbent paper.

The ink almost always penetrated this kind of paper which is the reason so many of these traditional style books require double-leaf pages (fukuro). This style of binding, called fukuro toji was adopted by the Japanese from the Chinese in the 14th century.

SIZE: 4¼" x 5½"

MATERIALS:
2 each 4¼" x 5½" of these papers (Pomegranate Salago, Orange Marmalade Salago, Grape Salago, Flannel Forest Salago)
36 sheets text paper 4¼" x 11" (Classic Solar White Linen)
4 White Unryu spine wraps 1⅛" x 4¼"
8 pieces Japanese Yuzen corner wraps ¾" x 1½"
4 pieces Yuzen title papers 1¼" x 3"
4 pieces Hosyo Professional White title papers 1" x 2¾"
5 hole-punching templates
1 yard unwaxed linen thread
20" Brown pearl cotton thread for 4-hole binding
26" Red pearl cotton thread for Kangxi binding
36" Lavender pearl cotton thread for Hemp Leaf binding
32" Blue pearl cotton thread for Tortoise Shell binding
1 Asian coin
1 Asian chopstick
18" Black grosgrain ribbon

SUPPLIES: Binder's needle • ¹⁄₁₆" hole punch • 8 small binder clips • *Akkra Inc.* teflon bone folder • Glue stick

INSTRUCTIONS:
Preparing the Text Blocks:
Fold the text papers in half to form pages that measure 4¼" x 5½". Note: In Japanese stab binding, the loose edges are bound, leaving the folds at the fore edge of the book. For this reason, a Teflon bone folder is an ideal tool because it doesn't leave shiny marks on the fold. If you do not have a Teflon bone folder, put a clean piece of paper over the fold before flattening with a regular bone folder to avoid leaving marks. Divide the papers into 4 equal groups of 9 sheets. Square up each of the 4 text blocks and secure with binder clips about 2" from the non-folded edge on the head and tail of the book blocks. Apply glue stick to 1 of the White unryu spine wraps and wrap it centered over the non-folded edge. Repeat for the other 3 text blocks. Cut out 5 templates. Line up the Inner Binding Template with the holes at the wrapped edge, and clamp it to the text block using the binder clips. Punch 2 pairs of ¹⁄₁₆" holes according to the template. Remove the template and re-clamp the text block. Repeat for the other 3 text blocks. Thread a needle with the unwaxed linen thread. Thread the needle through the first pair of holes and tie a Square knot. Clip the threads close to the knot. Repeat for all the other pairs of holes. This inner binding, called nakatoji, strengthens the book so that it won't come apart if the cover stitching breaks. It also makes handling the books easier during stitching. We are using unwaxed linen thread because it's fairly fine and strong.

instructions continue on pages 28-31

1. Fold the text weight paper in half and divide into 4 groups of 9. Do not nest.

2. Glue spine wrap around the edge opposite the fold.

3. Clip the template in place and punch inner binding holes.

continued from pages 26-27

Preparing the Text Blocks:

Traditional Japanese stab binding utilizes twisted paper string, Koyori, that is made by twisting a long strip of paper that's pounded flat after stitching with a mallet. We use a different template for this step so that the holes don't interfere with the outer binding.

Take 2 matching pieces of Yuzen paper measuring ¾" x 1½". Fold each one ½" in from a long end, right sides together. Clip the corners off the folded end leaving ¼" of the fold in the center. Apply glue stick to the wrong side of the paper and wrap it tightly around the first corner.
Hint: the fold goes in the corner; the short side of the wrap goes on the long side of the book. Repeat for the other corners of the text blocks. These corner wraps are called kadogire. When all 4 text blocks are prepared, it's time to sew.

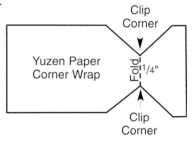

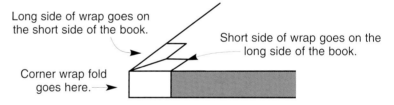

Sewing the Text Blocks:

Since the stitches build on each other and increase in difficulty, work the books in the following order:

4 Hole Binding: Pomegranate covers, brown thread, gold corners

Kangxi Binding: Orange Marmalade covers, red thread, blue and yellow corners

Hamp Leaf Binding: Grape covers, lavender thread, purple corners

Tortoise Shell Binding: Flannel Forest covers, blue thread, teal corners

Layer the covers over the outside of the text blocks and clamp into place. Add each template to the appropriate bound (sewing) edge of each book and clamp into place. Punch holes according to each template and remove the templates. Re-clamp. Begin with brown thread on the red book. To start, insert the threaded needle between the second and third pages and exit through 1 of the middle holes, leaving a 3" tail. Sew the book according to the drawings. When you finish the last stitch, bring the needle through the final hole and come back out between the 2nd and 3rd pages. Tie off with a square knot, clip the threads off short and tuck the knot close to the spine. Repeat for the other 3 books.

Lastly, stamp the pieces of Hosyo papers with Japanese characters. Attach each one to a piece of Yuzen paper. This is the title strip or diasen and is attached near the top of the fore edge of the front cover. Remember, Japanese books read opposite from Western-style books so the title strip actually is attached to what Westerners consider the back cover.

Steps 1-3 on page 27

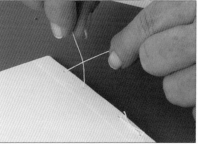

4. Tie the inner bindings for all four books.

5. Prepare the corner wraps.

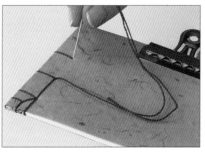

8. Sew the Orange book with the Kangxi binding stitch.

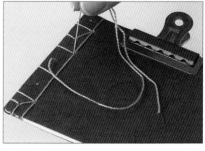

9. Sew the Purple book with a Hemp Leaf binding stitch.

Traditional Japanese books open from left to right, and are bound on the right. This Red book is traditionally Japanese... other star-bound books are pictured adapted for the Western tradition of opening right to left.

4-HOLE BINDING
(Yotsume Toji)

1.
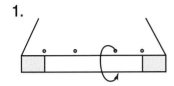

2.
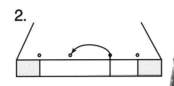

3.
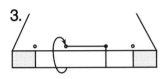

4.
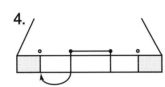

5.
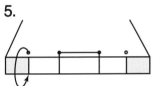

6.

7.
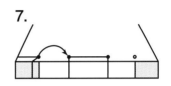

8.
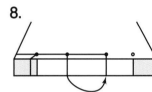

9.
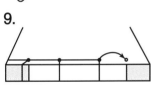

10.

11.

12.
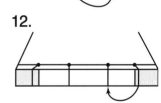

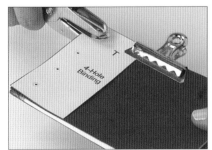

6. Add covers and punch outer binding holes for each book.

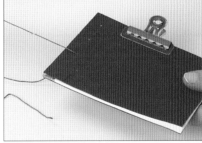

7. Sew the red book using the 4-hole binding stitch. See diagram.

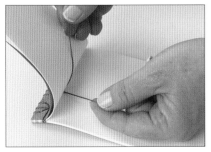

10. Sew the teal book using the Tortoise Shell binding stitch.

11. Stamp the titles and adhere to book with glue stick.

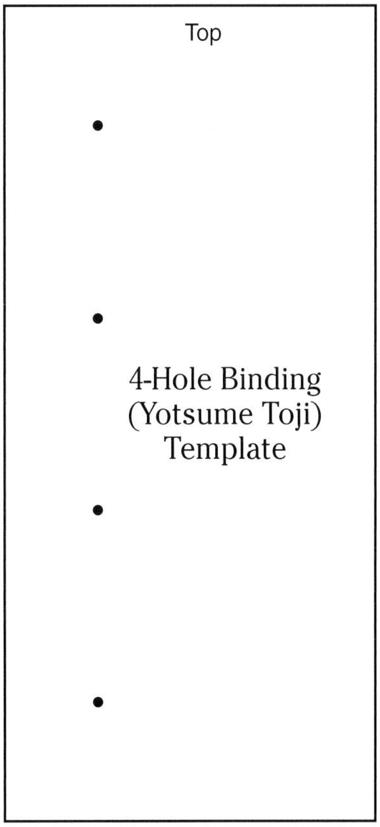

Top

4-Hole Binding
(Yotsume Toji)
Template

賀
夢
美
智
好

The Pillow Books of Lady Otori

continued from pages 28-29

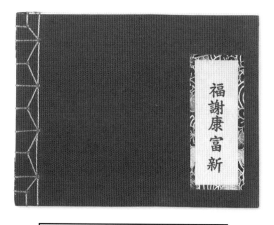

9.

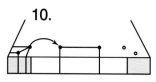

10.

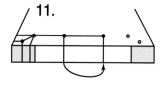

11.

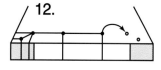

12.

Top

Kangxi
Binding
Template

Top

Hemp
Leaf
Binding
Template

13.

14.

15.

16.

17.

18.

KANGXI BINDING

Follow 4-Hole Binding until
completing step 6

7.

8.

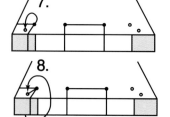

HEMP LEAF BINDING
(Asa-no-ha-Toji)

Follow Kangxi Binding until
completing step 18

19.

20.

21.

These traditional Japanese stab-bound books are known as 'makurabon' or pillow books due to their size and shape. They are made from half size oblong sheets of text paper.

Top

Tortoise Shell Binding Template

TORTOISE SHELL BINDING
(Kikko Toji)

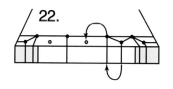

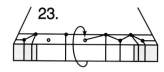

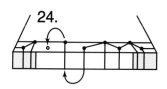

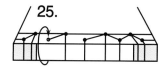

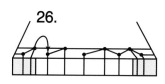

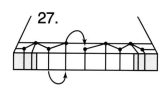

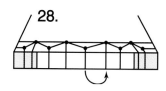

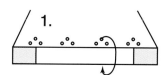

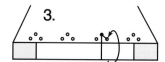

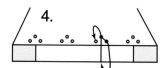

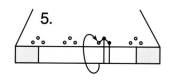

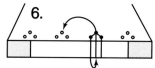

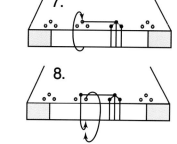

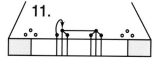

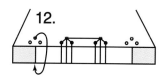

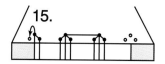

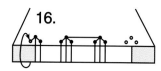

Tortoise Shell continued on page 32

continued from page 31

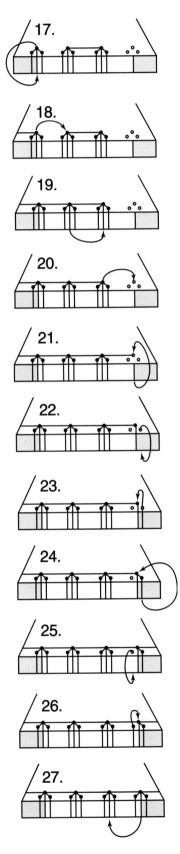

17.

18.

19.

20.

21.

22.

23.

24.

25.

26.

27.

Zig Zag Book

Have you ever had four family members record their impressions of the same event? This Zig Zag book provides space for four different stories - what a unique idea!

There are also many artistic themes that come in fours - the four points of the compass, the four seasons, or photos of your four children or siblings. Once you start thinking about it, the ideas just keep coming.

SIZE: 3¼" x 3¼" x 1"

MATERIALS:
8 pieces chipboard 3¼" square
3 sheets black cardstock 8½" x 11"
1 piece decorative paper 5½" x 11"
28 pieces ¾" x 1½" book cloth
24 sheets text paper 3" x 6"
2 yards *Royalwood Ltd.* waxed linen thread
2 hole-punching templates

SUPPLIES: Binding needle • Paper trimmer or craft knife and cutting mat • Scissors • PVA glue, glue stick

INSTRUCTIONS:

Making the cover assembly:

The first step is to make the book assembly using the chipboard squares and the book cloth strips. Template #1 is used to mark the spots where the strips will be adhered so that the books can be sewn in correctly. The easiest way to accomplish this task is to break it down into 4 pairs. Lay 2 pieces of chipboard side by side with a ¼" gap between them. Don't make the mistake of leaving a smaller gap or you will have trouble fitting your book into the space. Cut out template #1. Lay it down about ½" from the right edge of the piece on the left. Mark the 4 lines with a pencil. Lay the template about ½" from the left edge of the other square and mark the lines. Apply PVA glue to the back of the first cloth strip and apply the strip centered to the space between the first 2 lines on the pieces of chipboard. Apply a second strip between the second pair of lines. Flip the pair over and repeat with 2 more strips so that the assembly looks the same on both sides. Repeat this procedure with 3 more pairs of chipboard squares. If you lay these pairs in a pattern like the drawing, you can see where you have to put the remaining pairs of cloth strips – notice it forms a zig zag pattern when it's completed correctly.

Cut the black cardstock into 16 pieces measuring 3" square. You will have a bit left over. Save it for another project. Cut the decorative paper into 8 equal pieces measuring 2¾" square. You might find it easier to keep the pieces in order as you cut them to make assembly easier. Adhere the batik squares to the black squares using a glue

stick. Apply the glue carefully so that you don't tear the paper. When these 8 squares are complete, adhere them to the chipboard assembly using PVA glue. Try to adhere them in the same pattern as your original piece of decorative paper if your paper is patterned. When you finish the front covers, adhere the other 8 pieces of black cardstock to the reverse side of the assembly. Those will be your end papers. The 4 books will be sewn into each of the 4 horizontal pairs of chipboard pieces.

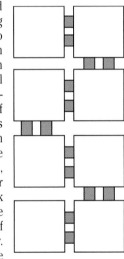

instructions continued on pages 34-35 templates on page 34

MAKE COVER, SPINE AND DECORATE SQUARES

1. Mark the chipboard using Template #1.

2. Glue book cloth strips to chipboard to make spines.

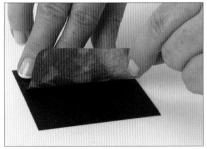

3. Glue decorative paper to the black squares.

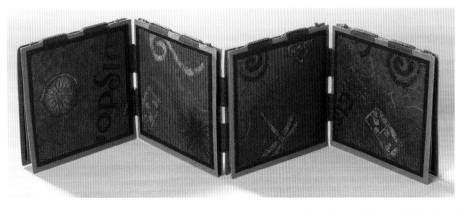

Zig Zag Book

continued from pages 32-33

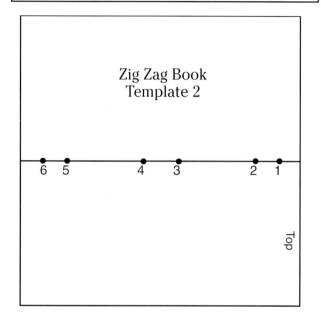

Sewing the Books:

Fold each of the 24 sheets of text paper in half to form sheets 3" x 3". Nest them in 12 signatures of 2 sheets each. Cut out the second template and score it down the middle. Mark the signatures with a T in the top right-hand corner. Since the signatures are only 2 sheets each, if you want to nest the signatures 3 at a time to punch the holes, you can. Then you'll only have to punch 4 times. If you do that, remember to separate the signatures into 2 sheets each again when you get ready to sew. To punch the holes, nest the template in the signature, making sure to match the Ts. Punch 6 holes according to the pattern. Repeat for the other signatures.

You will sew 3 signatures into each book. If you fold the assembly in half vertically, you can easily see the 4 sets of covers that you will be sewing into. Begin with the top pair of covers. Insert the first signature between the covers with the T on top. Cut the thread into 4 equal parts of 18" each. Thread your needle with the first piece. Begin on the outside of the book at the bottom (6th) hole of the signature. Insert your needle and pull the thread all the way through, leaving a tail of about 3". Come out the nearest hole (5th) in the signature. Insert your needle into the 4th hole and pull the thread all the way through. The thread will lay over the tape – hence the stitch name "Sewing over Tapes". Come out the signature at the 3rd hole, insert your needle into the second hole and come out at the 1st hole

at the top of the signature. Lay the second signature on top of the first so that they are flat against each other. Insert your needle into the 1st hole of the second signature. Sew in the same manner as you did the first signature until you exit the second signature at the bottom (6th) hole. Connect the first 2 signatures with a Square knot, right thread over left, then left over right. Trim the tail to ¹/₁₆". Lay the last signature on top of the first 2. Insert your needle into the 6th hole of the 3rd signature. Sew to the top of the signature in the same manner as the first signature. When you exit the 3rd signature at the 1st hole, connect the signatures with a half hitch knot and trim the thread to ¹/₁₆". To do a half hitch knot, insert your needle into the space where the thread connects the 1st and 2nd signatures. Pull until a loop forms and insert your needle into that loop. Pull the thread snugly until a knot forms.

Repeat this sewing for the other 3 books. When you are finished, fold the books together in a zig zag pattern. You may have to weight the book for a while to get it to lay flat.

Steps 1-3 on pages 32-33

4. Glue decorated paper to the chipboard.

5. Glue black squares to the reverse side of the chipboard assembly.

6. Fold text papers in half and punch holes using Template #2.

7. Sew 3 signatures into each book.

Keys to Wisdom

SUPPLIES: Teflon craft sheet • Non-stick craft iron • 2⅛" square Marvy Giga Punch • Sponge brush • *Tsukineko* (Terra Cotta Walnut ink, Bark Versacolor cube, Onyx Black Versafine ink) • Various rubber stamps: backgrounds and quotes • *Akkra Inc.* teflon bone folder • Awl • 2 pairs of flat-nosed jewelry pliers • Metal letters • Hammer and anvil • Black acrylic paint (Wisdom on brass washer) • PVA glue • Sponge brush • Glue stick

"Don't just live the length of your life, live the width as well." What a great quote for an accordion book! Keys to Wisdom is a delightful collection of thoughts for the day.

Look through each window to discover a different charming key to wisdom..

SIZE: 3½" x 3½" x 1⅛"

MATERIALS:

14 sheets Balsa cardstock 3⅜" x 6¾"	2 brass washers
2 pieces chip board 3⅜" square	1 piece copper wire 8"
2 pieces Lokta cover paper 5" square	4 fibers 16"
8 brass key charms	2 glass beads
7 brass jump rings	2 beige Velcro dots
1 charm fiber 24"	1 bead threader

INSTRUCTIONS:

Concertina pages:

In a shallow bowl, pour 2 teaspoons of the walnut ink. Dilute with ¼ cup of water. Crumple 7 sheets of Balsa cardstock into a wad and flatten out again slightly, leaving some wrinkles intact. Lay the first crumpled card on the Teflon craft sheet and dab with the walnut ink. Cover both sides of the cardstock with the ink solution and allow some of the ink to puddle slightly. Using a non-stick craft iron, iron all the wrinkles flat on both sides. (I place my craft sheet on a newsprint pad to protect my work surface.) After the cardstock sheets cool, fold each one in half to form sheets 3⅜" square. Flatten each again and stamp a quote in the center of each of the first 7 cards so that the fold line runs vertically down the center of

instructions continued on pages 38-39

1. Iron crumpled sheets flat. Fold in half.

2. Stamp each page in the center over the fold.

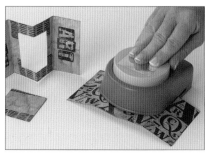

3. Punch a square from the center of each sheet.

4. Glue a cut-out to a stamped paper.

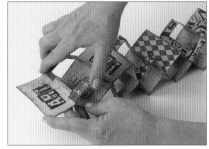

5. Glue back to back to make a concertina.

6. Thread the decorative cord through each fold.

Keys to Wisdom

continued from pages 36-37

each quote. Edge with a Bark Versacolor cube and set aside.

Crumple the other 7 Balsa cards, treat with walnut ink and iron each one. Stamp a different background stamp on each card using Onyx Black Versafine ink. Fold each one in half, wrong sides together, to form sheets measuring 3⅜" square. Now fold each edge of the card so that it meets the center fold, making a 4-panel card. Repeat for all 7 cards. Flatten the first card and insert it, with the stamped image facing away, into a 2⅛" square punch. For proper placement, it's best to set the punch on the table with the punch opening facing you. Guide the card so that the center fold of the card runs right down the middle of the punch opening. The card should be inserted into the punch as far as it will go. This will center the square perfectly according to the measurements of the card. Punch each card the same way.

Concertina Assembly:

Now you have 7 sets of quotes and 7 sets of backgrounds with square openings. The background cards will each have a mountain fold in the middle and 2 valley folds, 1 on either side of the mountain fold. The quote cards will just have a valley fold running down the center of the quote. Four of these panels will face forward and 3 will face backward. Take a minute to decide how you want to pair

them up, with 1 quote and 1 background in each pair. If you want, decide which pair will face which direction. Adhere each pair by applying glue stick to the 2 outside panels of the background card. Matching up the edges, press the background card onto the quote card until the glue starts to dry. Set each pair aside after you glue it. After all 7 pairs are glued, form the concertina booklet. Choose 4 glued cards to face forward and lay them side by side so that they form a line. Note that the line forms 4 mountain folds and 3 valley folds if looking from above the line of cards. Place the 3 remaining glued cards facing the opposite direction so that each one sits in a valley fold. You will attach the right panel of 1 card to the left panel of another to create the concertina. Apply PVA glue with a sponge brush to the right panel of the first glued pair and attach it to the left panel of the next and so on until the concertina is formed.

The next step is to run a strand of charm thread all the way through the concertina so that you have a line to dangle your key charms from. Imagine a line running from the beginning of the concertina to the end, about a ¼" from the top. Using an awl, gently poke holes about ¼" from the top of the concertina. The holes will run horizontally so that a thread can be drawn through them. Using the bead-threader, thread the

Steps 1-6 on page 36-37

7. Stamp the back cover.

8. Glue cover in place, sandwiching the fibers between the cover and end papers.

9. Affix closure to the cover with Velcro.

24" piece of charm thread through all 8 holes. Open the concertina as wide as you want it to open so that you have the thread placed correctly before you adhere the ends of the thread to the outside of the first and last panels with double-stick tape. Attach the key charms to the jump rings and jump rings to the thread so that each charm dangles in 1 of the openings. One of your keys will be a duplicate. Set that aside for your cover embellishment.

Apply glue stick to 1 chipboard cover. Lay the cover centered over the wrong side of the cover paper and press with a wad of waxed paper to adhere. Waxed paper can help you smooth out a paper as you glue to prevent wrinkles and eliminate the chance of dirtying your cover paper with your fingers. Miter the corners, apply glue stick and wrap the ends around the cover board. Repeat for the other cover. Stamp as you wish. You may want to use an alphabet set to stamp the words, "Keys to Wisdom" or just decorate with key stamps. Take the remaining 4 fibers and divide them into 2 groups. Attach the first 2 to the front cover using double-stick tape. Adhere the front cover using PVA glue applied with a glue brush. The fibers should be coming out the right side. Repeat for the back cover. In this case, the fibers will be coming out the same side as the front cover. Peel the backing off the fuzzy half of the Velcro dots and apply 1 to the fore edge of each front and back cover where the fibers are coming out.

Use ⅛" metal letter punches to hammer the word "Wisdom" into the edge of 1 of the washers. Dab with acrylic paint to highlight the letters. Wipe off the excess before it dries. Wrap the copper wire around the bottom half of the washer 3 times. Add the last key, and wrap another 3 times. Thread the end of the wire under the loops on the back of the washer to secure. The fibers coming out of the front cover will be wrapped around the back cover and secured to the front cover Velcro. Wrap the front cover fibers around the fore edge and the back cover and bring them around to the front again. Thread the fibers through the washer with the key, holding the washer over the spot where the Velcro dot is to gauge how tight to tie the fibers. Tie a double overhand knot with the fibers to secure the washer. Peel and stick the other half of the Velcro dot to the back of the washer, making sure to position the wire and threads properly before sticking. Repeat this process for the back cover fibers. To finish, thread 1 set of fibers through a glass bead and knot the fibers to secure the bead. Repeat for the other set of fibers. Wrap the fibers around the covers and attach the washers to close.

In this project you will learn 3 types of decorative spine binding. You will begin with a simple single signature binding called a *Chain Stitch*. Then you will progress to a slightly more challenging double-signature binding called *Crossed Snowshoes*.

Last, you will tackle a triple-signature binding called a *Spine Braid*. Because the spines are of differing widths, the first thing you will need to do is to choose which cover you want to use for each book and then trim the pieces of decorative scrapbook paper accordingly.

SIZE: 5½" x 8½"

MATERIALS:
3 sheets ivory cardstock 12" x 12"
3 sheets decorative scrapbook paper 12" x 12"
6 yards *Royalwood Ltd.* brown waxed linen thread
3 hole-punching templates for spines
3 hole-punching templates for signatures
60 sheets ivory text weight paper 8½" x 11"
3 brass label holders
Ivory cardstock for labels

Travel Journal Trio

Here are the correct measurements for each book:
1 signature book: 8⅝" x 11⅜"
2 signature book: 8⅝" x 11¾"
3 signature book: 8⅝" x 12"

SUPPLIES: 3" x 13" foam core board • 6 binding needles • Scissors • Craft knife • Cutting mat • Metal ruler • Bone folder • Awl • PVA glue and glue brush • *Zig* wide applicator 2 way glue • *Hermafix* temporary bond tape runner

INSTRUCTIONS:
Once you have the decorative papers cut to size, you'll need to bond it to cardstock to make sturdy covers. I recommend a Zig glue pen with a wide applicator for this job. Apply the glue to the back of the paper and adhere it to the cardstock. After the paper is firmly bonded to the cardstock, trim the cardstock to size with a craft knife and metal ruler. This is much easier than trying to match a sticky paper to the same size cardstock with precise accuracy.

The next step is to prepare the spines of your books. Gayle Burkins and Pam Sussman have devised a clever way to fold cover stock so that the spine will fall exactly in the center.

Take the cover stock measuring 11⅜" in width and put it in front of you with decorative paper facing the table and the long measurement laying horizontally. Measure ¼" in from both sides of the long edges. Make a pencil mark at each location. Now, bring the right side of the cardstock over to meet the 2 marks on the left side. Fold and make a sharp crease with a bone folder. Flatten out the cardstock. Repeat, bringing the left side over to the right marks and crease. This will give you a ¼" spine in the center of your cardstock. Nifty trick, isn't it?

Take the second piece of cardstock measuring 11¾" in width. Make pencil marks at ⅜" from both sides of the long edges. Fold and crease with a bone folder. Repeat for the other side. This will give you a ⅜" spine in the center of your cardstock.

Now, repeat this procedure with the third piece of 12" cardstock, making pencil marks at ⅝" from both sides. After folding, you will have a ⅝" spine in the center of your cardstock.

Trim all the hole punching templates. Choose the 3 labeled Spine Hole-Punching Templates and make 2 score marks vertically on each where designated. When you fold these templates, they should fit snugly into the spines of your covers. Use a Hermafix temporary glue bond to keep them in place while you punch holes in the spines with an awl according to each template. Hint: Use a piece of foam core board under your spine to make punching easier. Mark each cover with a T in pencil on the inside of the cover to designate the top.

Next, prepare the signatures by folding the text weight paper in half and nesting in groups of 10 sheets per signature. Mark each signature with a T in the top right corner to designate the top. Score all the signature hole-punching templates and fold in half vertically. Find the Chain stitch template for the single-signature book and punch 1 signature using an awl. Remember to match the T of the signature with the T in the template. Find the Crossed Snowshoes template for the 2-signature book and punch 2 signatures using an awl. Finally, use the Spine braid template to punch 3 signatures for the last book.

Now for the fun part – stitching!

instructions continue on pages 42-44

COVERS, SPINE, SIGNATURES AND STITCH BINDING

1. Fold paper for each book cover.

2. Punch holes in the spine using the spine template.

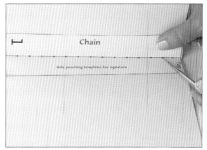
3. Punch holes in the signatures using the template.

4. Sew a single-signature book using the Chain stitch.

5. Sew a double-signature book using the Crossed Snowshoes stitch.

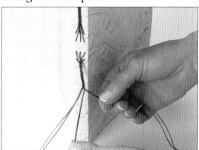
6. Sew the triple-signature book using the Spine Braid stitch.

Travel Journal Trio

instructions continued from pages 40-41

Book #1 – The Chain Stitch

Thread a binder's needle with 1 yard of brown waxed linen thread. Take your single signature cover and nest its corresponding signature inside with the Ts matching. Begin on the inside at the 1st station. Insert the needle and pull the thread through, leaving a 3" tail. Insert the needle into the hole at the 2nd station. Tie off with a square knot inside and trim the tail to ⅛" before coming back out the 1st station. Re-enter the signature at the 2nd station.

Now that you have completed the beginning chain stitch, the chain stitch will be repeated until you tie off at the end. Exit the signature at the 3rd station. Take your needle and slip it under the 2 threads which are coming out of the 2nd station. Re-enter the 3rd station. Repeat this stitch until you exit the bottom station. At this point, make a half hitch knot to tie off the thread. To do a half hitch, slip your needle through the thread on the inside of the signature which is between the last 2 stations. Pull the thread until a loop forms. Slip the needle through the loop, pull snugly to form a knot. Trim the thread to ⅛".

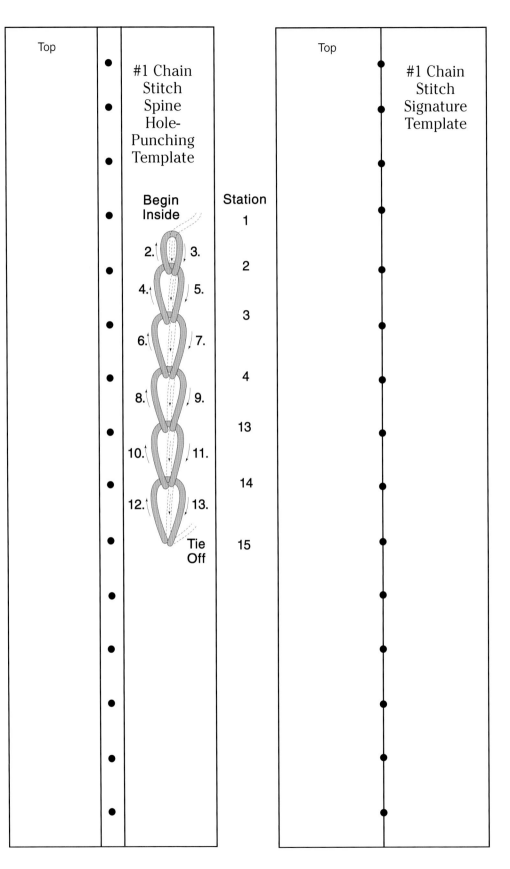

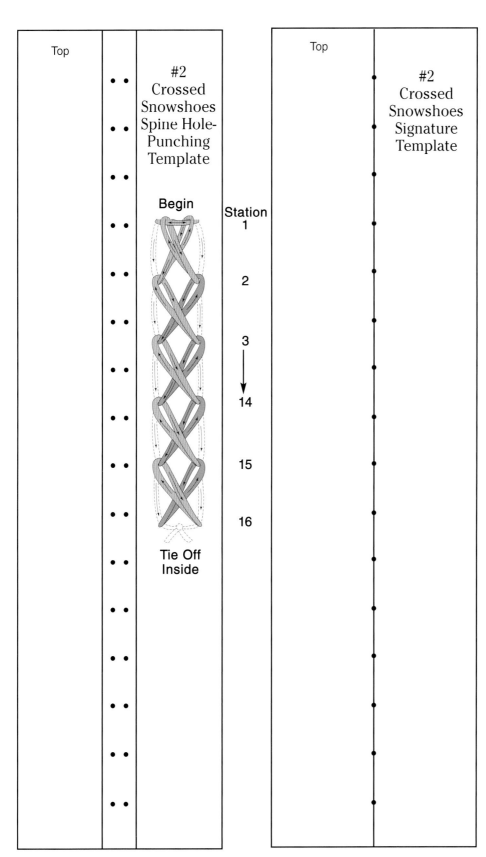

Top

#2
Crossed
Snowshoes
Spine Hole-
Punching
Template

Begin

Station
1

2

3

↓

14

15

16

**Tie Off
Inside**

Top

#2
Crossed
Snowshoes
Signature
Template

Rome

Book #2 – Crossed Snowshoes

This stitch is really just a double chain stitch sewn with 2 needles. Begin by threading 2 yards of Brown waxed linen thread with a needle at each end. Take the double signature cover and nest the corresponding signatures inside, matching the Ts of the cover with those on the signatures. Find the midpoint of your thread by matching up the ends of the thread and making a pinch in the middle. Insert a needle into each of the 2 holes at the outside of the first station. Pull the thread through, making sure the 'pinch' falls between the 2 holes. Exit each signature at the 2nd station.

Starting with the left thread, slip the needle over the right side of the thread connecting the top 2 holes. Re-enter the signature through the left hole of the 2nd station. Repeat this procedure with the right needle, looping it over the connection thread on the left side. Re-enter the signature through the right hole at the 2nd station. Exit each signature at the 3rd station. Repeat the crossed snowshoes stitch until you reach the last station. Remember to start with the same needle at each station so the threads cross in the same way each time for consistency. When you get to the last station, you will loop the threads in the same manner but only re-enter the cover with each needle – not the signatures. When both threads are on the inside of the cover, tie off with a square knot.

INSTRUCTIONS:
Book #3 – Spine Braid

The Spine Braid stitch is a little trickier because you will be working with 6 needles. Don't let this intimidate you. This is a simple stitch – just a little awkward at times.

You will begin the 3 rows of threads at the outside of each signature. Take three 1-yard pieces of brown waxed linen and thread a needle onto the ends of each piece. Find the midpoint of each piece the same way you did in Book #2. Insert the first signature into the spine, matching up the Ts. Insert each needle, one at a time into the spine and signature from the outside. Pull the thread evenly until the midpoint of the thread is close to the spine, forming a loop. Then bring both needles over the top of the book and through the loop at the midpoint of the thread. Pull the loop from inside the signature until it rests against the spine. Pull the descending threads until they are snug. **Figure 1** shows what the result should look like. Repeat for the other 2 signatures.

At this point you should have 6 needles and 6 strands of thread dangling on the outside of the spine but don't let this overwhelm you. Pair up each vertical row so that you have 3 pairs of 2 threads. Braid them until you reach the 2nd station. Separate each pair into 2 threads again, starting with the pair on the left. Re-enter the signature with 1 of the 2 threads at station 2 and the other thread at station 3 in the row on the left. Repeat for second pair in center row of holes at stations 2 and 3 and for the last pair of threads in right row of holes at stations 2 and 3.

To exit each signature, take the thread at station 2 and exit the signature at station 4. Take the thread at station 3 and exit the signature at station 5. Repeat for the other 2 signatures.

Combine each pair again and braid until you reach the 6th station. Re-enter the signatures at stations 6 and 7. Exit the signatures at stations 8 and 9, repeating the procedures above. Braid 1 more time but do not enter the last set of holes. Instead, begin with the pair of threads on the left side of the spine to tie off. Wrap both threads over the tail (bottom) of the book, laying the threads next to each other rather than on top of each other. Exit the last station with only 1 of the needles. Wrap the thread over the pair of threads on the spine and re-enter the signature. Tie off the pair with a square knot. Repeat this tie off for the other 2 signatures.

Add embellishments to the covers as desired.

#3 Spine Braid Hole-Punching Template	Top

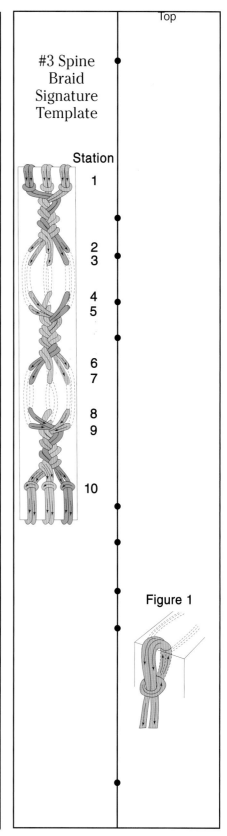

#3 Spine Braid Signature Template

Station

1
2
3
4
5
6
7
8
9
10

Figure 1

SIZE: 5⅛" x 6¼"

MATERIALS:
1 piece book board 5" x 6¼"
1 piece book board 1" x 6¼"
1 piece book board 3¾" x 6¼"
2 pieces handmade cover paper 7" x 8¼"
2 pieces end paper 4¾" x 6"
40 sheets handmade text paper
Hole-punching template
1 piece Tyvek 1" x 14"
6" stick
36" hemp cord
Various decorative leaves

SUPPLIES: ⅛" hole punch • PVA glue

Nature Journal

A variety of textures makes this book a joy to touch. This book is a natural gift choice for anyone who loves journals. The handmade papers are incredibly soft. This binding style is simple to do and a good one to use when the book does not need to open flat.

continued on page 46

NATURE COVERS, PAGES & BINDING

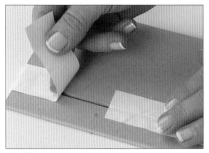

1. Wrap the front cover hinge in Tyvek.

2. Punch holes in covered boards.

3. Punch holes in text paper.

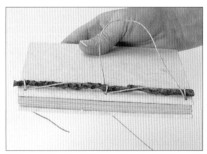

4. Sew the book following instructions.

5. Embellish the cover with dried leaves or flowers.

INSTRUCTIONS:

Top

○ 1   ○ 2

Nature
Journal
Template

○ 3   ○ 4

5   6
○   ○

Cover the piece of book board that measures 5" x 6¼" using 1 of the pieces of handmade cover paper and PVA glue. Apply PVA glue to the wrong side of the end paper and adhere the end paper to the inside of the cover board. The next 2 pieces of book board that measure 1" and 3¾" in width will be laid side by side with a ¼" gap between them to form the front cover. Using PVA glue, adhere the Tyvek to the ¼" gap between the front cover boards. The added Tyvek will make a stronger hinge than the cover paper alone. Use the other piece of cover paper to cover this assembly. Adhere the other end paper to the inside of the front cover. Clamp the cover template to the front cover and punch 6 holes in the 1" wide piece of the cover assembly. Remove the template and clamp it to the inside of the back cover and punch 6 holes in that also. Clamp the text weight paper together in small groups with the template on top and punch holes in each group until all the pages are punched.

Sandwich the text paper inside the front and back covers and clamp with a large bulldog clamp. Lay the stick between the 2 rows of holes. If you have a needle with a large enough eye, thread it with the hemp cord. If not, a dental floss threader will do the trick just as well. Begin the stitching on the back of the book block and enter at the first hole at the head of the book, leaving a tail to tie off. Check the template for the hole numbers. Think of this stitch as a giant cross stitch. Wrap the hemp cord over the stick and enter the 2nd hole at the head of the book. Re-enter the 1st hole and pull the cord through the hole to the front of the book. Cross over the stick at a diagonal and enter the 4th hole. Pull the cord through to the back of the book and enter the 3rd hole. Pull the cord through to the front of the book and re-enter the 4th hole, wrapping the cord over the stick. Re-enter the 3rd hole and pull the cord back through to the front. Wrap the cord diagonally over the stick and enter the 6th hole. Pull the thread through the back of the book and enter the 5th hole. Wrap the cord over the stick and re-enter the 6th hole. Pull the cord through to the back and re-enter the 5th hole. Wrap the cord diagonally over the stick and enter the 4th hole. Pull the cord through to the back and enter the 3rd hole. Wrap the cord diagonally over the stick and enter the 2nd hole. Tie off on the back of the book with a square knot.

Decorate the cover using a variety of dried leaves and/or flowers. Hint: for skeleton leaves and other delicate flora, consider using Xyron adhesive. Peel the backing away from the leaf, as opposed to peeling the leaf away from the backing. This will prevent the leaf from crumbling.

There is so much you can do with metal that it is really fun to work with.
Metal also makes a very sturdy cover for this wonderful book that also opens flat.

SIZE: 4¼" x 5⅝"

MATERIALS:

2 pcs. 5¼" x 6½" 36 gauge aluminum
2 pcs. 4¼" x 5½" matboard
2 pcs. 4⅛" x 5⅜" black felt
8 Silver ⅛" long reach eyelets

16 sheets 8½" x 11" Beckett Enhance Marble Grey paper
2 pieces 36" Black waxed linen thread
1 cover hole-punching template
1 signature hole-punching template

SUPPLIES: *Deja Views* 3" stencil Spunky font • *Ten Seconds Studio* Tooling pad with acrylic on one side; Metal tools: Teflon-tipped stylus, refiner tool, ball and cup, decorative wheels, paper stump • Metal letters, hammer, bench block • Lightweight spackle • Black acrylic paint • 4 binder's needles • Bone folder • ⅛" hole punch and eyelet setter • Awl • Waxed paper • PVA glue

INSTRUCTIONS: ***Tooling the front cover:*** You will be working with 36 gauge aluminum. It is thin and brittle, but soft enough to work. A better alternative is pewter which is much softer and more pliable; however, it is about twice the cost of aluminum. Learning to work aluminum first will make pewter seem like a dream, so let's begin! Select a letter and a theme for your book. You may use your first initial and your name or choose a concept instead. Lay the tooling pad soft side up. Position the stencil on the metal in reverse, centered right to left, and about 1¾" from the top of the metal. Trace the letter with the Teflon-tipped tool. Remember, this is thin aluminum and you can punch a hole in it if you put too much pressure on it. • **Defining the letter**: After tracing, flip the pad over to the hard acrylic side. With refiner tool, trace the letter on both sides of the line you made to define the letter clearly. • **Divide the letter into sections**: Lay tooling pad with padded side up. Position the letter in reverse. Use the Teflon-tipped tool to divide the letter into sections of straight or wavy lines. Define the sections the same way you defined the original letter. • **Decorating each section**: Using the padded side of your tooling pad, with the letter facing in reverse, press the ball-end of the ball and cup tool into the metal and rotate it gently. Now flip the pad over to the hard side and the metal over also so that the letter is facing the correct direction. Using the other end of the tool, press the cup over the round indentation that the ball made. It automatically defines the ball perfectly. Use several different sizes of ball and cup tools in 1 section of your let-

Dream Journal Cover Template

Top

ter. • For the next section, place the padded side of the tooling pad up. Position the letter facing up. Use several different wheels to roll across the metal so a pattern emerges. • On the other sections, with the letter facing up and the padded side of the tooling pad up, use a stylus to make small swirls, a basketweave pattern, or a crosshatch pattern. Define it the same way on the reverse side of the metal, but also press the little squares forward on the right side with the Teflon tip to give it more dimension. • **Emboss the Word**: Use the padded side of the tooling pad. Stamp the word with metal letters and a hammer. • **Add dimension to the letter**: Reverse the letter and place it on the padded side of the tooling pad. Use a paper stump tool. Begin in 1 corner and gently press the letter by rubbing back and forth. Do not put too much pressure on the metal. Repeated gentle pressure will give you the results you want without obliterating the design. • **Fill the letter**: To maintain the shape of the letter, fill it with spackle and smooth it so that it is completely level. Dry overnight. • **Antiquing**: Spread Black acrylic paint over the front of the metal. Wait a minute and then rub the excess off. Don't wait too long or rub too hard!

Tooling the back cover: Impress your

instructions continued on page 48

TRANSFER PATTERN, SPACKLE DESIGN, PUNCH HOLES AND BIND BOOK

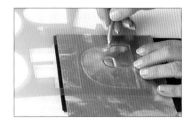

1. Trace the "D" in reverse on metal.

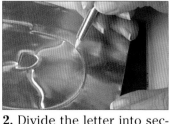

2. Divide the letter into sections to be decorated.

3. Detail each section.

4. Puff the design forward and fill with spackle.

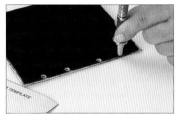

5. Punch holes in the cover.

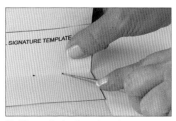

6. Punch holes in signatures using a template.

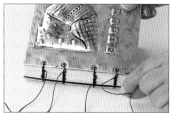

7. Sew the binding.

Dream Journal
Signature Template   Top

initials into the bottom portion of the metal using metal stamps, a hammer and a bench block. Texture the rest of the metal in the same manner you textured the front cover of your book.

Preparing the covers: Center the front piece of aluminum over a piece of matboard. Miter the corners, leaving a margin equal to the thickness of the board in all 4 corners. Apply PVA glue to the matboard and press the matboard centered onto the back of the aluminum. Burnish with a wad of waxed paper. Fold the 2 opposite sides of the aluminum over. Press the folds with a bone folder, paying special attention to the corners. Be sure to flatten the little bit of corners that overlap so that your next folds will be smooth. Fold over the other 2 flaps and burnish. • Apply PVA glue to the back side of the matboard and folded aluminum flaps, avoiding the last ⅛" of the edges. Apply a felt piece, centered over the matboard and press to secure. Repeat this procedure for the back cover aluminum. • **Binding holes**: Cut out the Cover template. Punch four ⅛" holes according to the pattern. Set 4 long reach eyelets in the holes. Repeat for the back cover. Your covers are now complete.

Preparing the signatures: Cut each text paper in half to 5½" x 8½". Fold each text paper in half to 4¼" x 5½". Sharpen each of the creases with a bone folder and nest the sheets into 8 signatures of 4 sheets each. Mark each signature with a T in the top right-hand corner to indicate the top. Cut out the signature template, mark the fold with a bone folder and fold it in half with the markings on the inside. Nest the template inside the first signature, making sure to match the Ts of the signature and template. Punch 4 holes according to the pattern. Repeat for the other 7 signatures.

Sewing the book block: Thread a needle onto each end of both pieces of waxed linen thread. You will be sewing the book from the back to the front. Each length of thread will be used to sew 1 of the pairs of holes in your book. Find the midpoint of each thread and make a pinch. Take your last signature and place it on the table in front of you, with the T on your left facing up. Thread each needle pair through each pair of holes from the inside to the outside of the signature so that the center of the thread is in the middle of each pair of holes. You will have 4 needles hanging outside at this point. • **Lock on the back cover:** Place the cover face down, lay the last signature on top. Start with the thread on your right. Wrap it around the cover and thread the needle through the first hole in the cover. When you come up through the hole, wrap the thread according to **Fig. A**. Repeat for remaining needles. The threads should fall to the inside of each pair of holes. • **Add a Signature:** Be sure the T on each signature is on your left facing up when you stack it over the previous one. Thread each needle into the hole directly above it and back out the opposite hole in the pair (See **Fig. B**). The thread should be snug but not so tight that it will pull or tear the holes in your signature. You want to be able to see the braid and if you pull too tightly, the braid will close up. • With the first

needle on the right, skip 1 signature below and wrap the thread according to **Fig. C**, threading from right to left. The next needle will wrap in the same manner but in the opposite direction – from left to right. Notice that the threads fall to the center of the holes. Repeat for the other pair of holes. • **Add remaining signatures**: Repeat the steps for adding and securing signatures until you finish the crossover on the last signature. • **Attach front cover:** Place the front cover on top of the first signature. Starting with the first needle on the right, wrap the thread over the cover and thread the needle through the first hole. Wrap it around the ascending thread going from right to left according to **Fig. D**. Repeat for the next hole

in the pair but wrap the thread from left to right. Note that the threads fall to the outside of the holes for the first time during the stitching. Repeat the procedure for the other pair of holes. • To secure the cover, skip 2 signatures down and wrap the first thread on your right through the ascending thread from right to left and insert the needle into the first hole of the first signature. Wrap the second thread around the ascending thread from left to right and insert the needle into the second hole of the first signature. Tie off the threads on the inside with a Square knot and clip the threads to ¼". Repeat the procedure for the other pair.

SEWING BOOKS TOGETHER

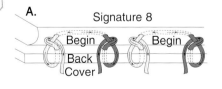

A. Signature 8
Begin   Begin
Back
Cover

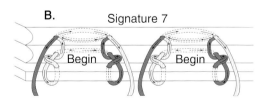

B. Signature 7
Begin   Begin

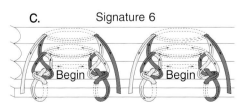

C. Signature 6
Begin   Begin

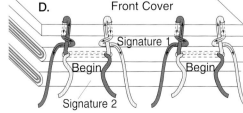

D. Front Cover
Signature 1
Begin   Begin
Signature 2

This book is one of the most innovative in this collection for the binding is constructed with safety pins and tubing. However, what makes this book really special is the sentiment it offers. "This is my wish for you... Comfort on difficult days, Smiles when sadness intrudes, Rainbows to follow the clouds, Laughter to kiss your lips, Hugs when spirits sag, Sunsets to brighten your being, Friendships to warm your heart, Beauty for your eyes to see, Faith so that you can believe, Confidence for when you doubt, Patience to know yourself, Courage to accept the truth, and always, Love to complete your life."

1. Trace and score the envelope template.

2. Insert safety pins into reinforced holes.

3. Trim open end with deckle scissors.

4. Decorate the envelope with with rub-on letters.

5. Stamp tags.

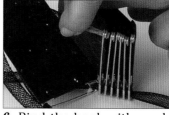

6. Bind the book with mesh tubing.

7. Connect tubing ends with crimp beads.

Mary Kaye Seckler

I would like to thank the artists whose work has inspired the pieces in this book: Leslie McFarlane, whose Lost and Found words spoke volumes to me; Terry Whinery, whose lovely little accordion pin showed me that books can be wearable; Pam Sparks, who shared her great ideas for polyshrink spirals; Donna Goss, who made a complicated concertina easy; Kathy Martin, who taught me a new way to look at an old stitch with the Zig Zag book; Cheryl Darrow, who taught me that metal is a fantastic art medium; and of course, Pam Sussman and Gayle Burkins, who taught me everything else I know about the art of bookbinding.

I thank my patient and talented husband, Bob Seckler, for the precise drawings and templates. Only he knows how many times some drawings had to be revised to reflect my artistic flights of fancy.

SUPPLIERS - Most craft and variety stores carry an excellent assortment of supplies. If you need something special, ask your local store to contact the following companies.

M. K. Seckler, www.artandsoulstudio.net
Akkra Inc., 585-506-6605, Rochester, NY
Clearsnap, 888-448-4862, Anacortes, WA
Hero Arts, 800-822-4376, Emeryville, CA
Inkadinkado, 800-888-4652, Reading, PA
JudiKins, 310-515-1115, Gardena, CA
Limited Edition Rubber Stamps, 888-782-6798, San Carlos, CA
Lucky Squirrel, 800-462-4912, Belen, NM
On the Surface, 847-675-2520, Wilmette, IL
Penny Black, 510-849-1883, Berkeley, CA
Postmodern Design, 405-321-3176, Norman, OK
Ranger Industries, 800-244-2211, Tinton Falls, NJ
ReadySet Tools, 801-292-6164, Centerville, UT
Royalwood Ltd., 800-526-1630, Mansfield, OH
Stampers Anonymous, 800-945-3980, Cleveland, OH
Ten Seconds Studio, www.tensecondsstudio.com
The Moon Rose Art Stamps, 631-549-0199, Huntington, NY
Tsukineko, 800-769-6633, Redmond, WA
Uchida, 800-541-5877, Torrance, CA

MANY THANKS to my friends for their cheerful help and wonderful ideas!
Kathy McMillan • Jennifer Laughlin
Patty Williams • Marti Wyble
Donna Kinsey
David & Donna Thomason

Rainbow Wish Book

SIZE: 2⅛" x 4½" x 1½"

MATERIALS:
Decorative paper for 14 envelopes
14 pieces cardstock 3" x 4" in rainbow colors
14 matching 12" fibers
14 large brass safety pins
1 piece black plastic mesh tubing 15"
20 black plastic pony beads
2 large brass crimp beads
2 large bore brass tube beads

SUPPLIES:
JudiKins coin envelope template • *Deluxe* Tag Template (#3T) • Awl • Scissors • Bone folder • ¼" hole punch • *Avery* clear hole reinforcement labels • Small (⅜") alphabet stamp alphabet • Decorative rubber stamp • *Tsukineko* (Versafine Onyx Black inkpad; Versacolor cubes for edging tags) • *Chatterbox* White alphabet rub-ons (Heber type) • Pliers • Deckle-edge scissors • 2 hemostats • Brush on Krazy glue

INSTRUCTIONS:
Trace the envelope template 14 times on the decorative paper and cut out. With a bone folder, score on the score lines indicated on the template. Fold on the long sides and then on the short end. Re-open envelope and punch 2 holes in the fold of the small flap about a half inch from each end of the fold. Stick a hole reinforcement label over each hole to prevent tearing. Insert a brass safety pin into the holes and close the pin. Apply glue stick on the long flap and seal it. Apply glue stick to the end flap and seal it with the pin in the fold. Use deckle-edged scissors to trim the flap off the open end of the envelope. Repeat for all envelopes.

Use white rub-ons on the envelope to put the beginnings of a wish. Repeat for all envelopes.

Trace the curved tag on the template on each of the 14 colors of cardstock. If you want to have a rainbow effect in the book, remember the order of the colors of the rainbow: Red, Orange, Yellow, Green, Blue, Indigo and Violet. (I used a dark shade and a light shade of each color for a total of 14 tags.) Cut out and punch a ¼" hole in the curved end of each. I stamped a decorative stamp at the curved end of each tag to unify the tags. Stamp a greeting that will clarify each of your wishes. Be creative!

When all the tags are stamped, add a color-coordinated fiber to each tag. Don't insert tags into the envelopes until the binding step is finished.

Cut the mesh tubing in half and miter 1 end of each length. Put the envelopes in the desired order. Pinch the tubing and thread the first piece through the top hole of each of the pins. Thread the other piece through the bottom hole of the pins. Center each piece of tubing. Slide 5 black pony beads into each of the 4 ends of the tubing.

Slide the large hole brass tube bead over one end of the tubing. Pinch the end of the tubing and attach a hemostat to the end to keep it closed. Attach another hemostat to the other end of tubing. Put the ends together and brush super glue over the ends to connect. Allow it to dry. Put a crimp bead over the seam in the tubing and clamp shut with pliers. Slide the large hole brass bead over the crimp bead. Repeat to seal the other piece of tubing. You can slide the tubing through the pins to center the brass beads.

Insert the tags into the corresponding envelopes. Your wish book is now complete.